D0776861

FROM AMOURETTE TO ŻAL

FROM AMOURETTE TO ŻAL

BIZARRE AND BEAUTIFUL WORDS FROM EUROPE
(FOR WHEN ENGLISH JUST WON'T DO)

ALEX RAWLINGS

The
History
Press

To my parents, who first gave me the gift of life and then passed on to me their love for language.

Acknowledgements

With special thanks to Fanny Thalén, Eustacia Vye, Zsófi Geschwendtner and Gaston Dorren for help and linguistic insights.

First published 2018

The History Press
The Mill, Brimscombe Port
Stroud, Gloucestershire, GL5 2QG
www.thehistorypress.co.uk

© Alex Rawlings, 2018

British Library Cataloguing in Publication Data.
A catalogue record for this book is available from the British Library.

ISBN 978 0 7509 8773 8

Typesetting and origination by The History Press
Printed and bound in Great Britain by TJ International Ltd

Contents

A World Without Grenzen

Die Grenzen meiner Sprache bedeuten
die Grenzen meiner Welt
The borders of my language signify
the borders of my world

Ludwig Wittgenstein, Austrian-British philosopher

The Wittgenstein quotation that opens this book is one that you might see regularly nowadays, popping up in internet memes, blogs, newspapers, and anything connected to language, learning languages, and multilingualism. However, if you have seen it before, you may remember a slightly different version of it. Conventionally, in English we tend to translate the German as: 'The limits of my language are the limits of my world.' Usually, there is no mention of the word 'borders' or 'signify', although broadly speaking the meaning of the two is still fairly close.

We understand in either version what Wittgenstein means. He is drawing attention to the fact that we can only truly know something if we have the language to describe it. If we don't have a precise word for something, we simply put it under the umbrella of the most similar object we do have a word for. That is why, for example, English sees dark blue and light blue as two shades of the same colour, but red and pink as different. Russian, on the other hand, has two separate names for the two colours: синий (*síniy*) is dark blue and голубой (*galubóy*) is light blue. For Russian speakers, this is not only a difference of vocabulary. They consider the two to be separate colours.

Yet Wittgenstein's choice of words in the German original is intriguing. Wittgenstein talks about *Grenzen*, which is primarily the German word for 'borders'. It can be translated as 'limit', but only in specific circumstances. To do so is problematic, because German has two words for 'limit', where English has one. German distinguishes between a natural limit and an artificially imposed limit. The maximum speed that a human being can ever run at is a *Grenze*, while the maximum speed at which a car is legally allowed to travel on a road is a *Begrenzung*.

Importantly, in German the word *Grenzen* takes on far more significance than its translations would for most English speakers. A German speaker residing in Germany, Switzerland or Austria is surrounded by national borders on all sides. Certain generations will remember what life was like before the Schengen agreement of 1995, when cars were forced to queue for hours before they could cross to the other side, waiting for their documentation to be checked by the *Grenzschutz*, or 'border control'. For half of the twentieth century, Germany itself even had a *Grenze* running down the middle of it, as the country was divided into East and West, with families and livelihoods severed on either side of the line.

To translate *Grenzen* as 'limits' in this case does not even come close to addressing the nuance that the word carries in German. So much meaning is lost, as unfortunately is always the case when we just look to the translation and ignore the original.

In the twenty-first century, English has become one of the most powerful languages in the world. It is hard to put a reliable estimate on just how many people worldwide speak it and to what degree, but undoubtedly it is the international language for business, tourism, politics, academia and almost all scenarios in which people from different countries need to communicate. The current trend is for this to increase, which means that wherever you go, there's an ever greater chance that you'll find someone able to speak and understand English.

Most native English speakers can hardly believe their luck. Through no achievement of their own, they are now able to cruise around speaking their language and feel as though everyone is able to understand them. As a result, all over the English-speaking world, people have stopped learning foreign languages. Those with traumatic memories of failing French tests at school now feel increasingly vindicated that 'it was all a waste of time'. Nowadays, even French president Emanuel Macron is happy to use English at press conferences, in stark contrast to his staunchly Francophone predecessors.

There are a number of reasons why this prevailing attitude is not only mistaken, but even damaging.

Firstly, although from an Anglophone point of view the world is becoming increasingly English speaking, from a global point of view the world is actually becoming more multilingual. Thanks to easier access to international media through the internet, an unprecedented boom in international travel and heightened awareness of the importance of doing business with other countries, more and more people around the world are learning to speak another language. It's just that the language they're learning happens to be English.

Multilingualism around the world is becoming the norm, and scientific research is showing incredible data about its health effects. The mental gymnastics required to pick up another tongue have already been proven to greatly increase cognitive abilities among multilingual people. In 2013, a report published in the journal *Neurology* showed people who spoke more than one language – including those who learned one later in life – even delayed the onset of dementia by four and a half years on average, compared with monolingual people.

So long as the cultural attitude persists that, because English speakers have somehow won the 'linguistic lottery of life', they are exempt from the need to learn other languages, how will they reap those benefits? Meanwhile, in other countries around the world the ability to speak more than one language is increasingly becoming as commonplace as literacy and typing skills were a hundred years ago.

Secondly, there is always a risk of assuming people are learning *your* English. The reality is most people probably aren't. They're learning their own English. They're keeping their own language and swapping out words for English equivalents, while strongly retaining their own identity and perspective on the world. Before our eyes, brand new dialects of English are springing up everywhere, which are already leaving native English speakers as baffled as if they were being spoken to in a foreign language.

People's native languages don't simply disappear when they start learning another language. They remain a constant reference point for whenever they need to express themselves in any language and will always strongly influence the way they speak them.

That's why, for example, Greek speakers often start questions in English with the word 'maybe', because they're searching for an equivalent for the word μήπως (*mípos*), which is always used to start a polite and formal question. 'Maybe you would like something to drink?' is a word-for-word translation of the Greek phrase 'Μήπως θα θέλατε κάτι να πιείτε;' ('*Mípos tha thélate káti na pyíte?*').

That's why French speakers often ask questions without changing the word order. Although it might sound rude or presumptuous in English, in French you don't have to, and it's perfectly acceptable not to. 'You would like the bill?' is a word-for-word translation of the French equivalent: '*Vous voudriez l'addition?*'

The third problem is the nature of languages themselves, which Wittgenstein's quotation alludes to more specifically. Languages are a constantly evolving, adapting and changing phenomenon that have come about over many generations. They are essentially mutually agreed sound systems that are attached to specific objects, actions, feelings and so on, but without having any particular correlation to the things that they describe. They tell the story of the people that speak them. They are a way to capture knowledge and pass experiences down through the generations.

We all share one planet, and, although the problems we face may not differ enormously between peoples and cultures, the ways in which we've come to talk about them do. Different languages are more or less perceptive about different things, depending on the environments in which they have come to evolve. That is why so many Greek idioms and expressions relate to the sea, as the whole country is essentially built along the shore and has relied on ships for thousands of years. It's perhaps also a reason why Russian idioms focus so much on mysticism and superstition, as what else could you do in Russia's long, dark and freezing winters other than stay inside, keeping warm around the stove and telling each other stories?

By never venturing outside the very large and comfortable bubble that is the English language, we never come into contact with the rich knowledge and challenging perspectives that other cultures have come to collect on our shared world. Or if we do, we'll have to approach it through translation, which as discussed causes problems of its own.

As the world becomes more multilingual and more open, English speakers around the world who cling on to their monolingualism ultimately run the risk of ending up quite isolated. Already we have seen political trends in both the UK and the USA that seem to be going in quite the opposite direction to the rest of the world, towards more isolationism, more protectionism and more exceptionalism. Perhaps, in a world where everyone seems to be able to speak our language but we can't speak theirs, we just don't feel special any more.

The point of this book, however, is not to offer political commentary. This book was written to celebrate the endless wealth of languages and multilingualism that we are so lucky to have in this world. With the help of many friends around the world, to whom I am extremely grateful, I have gathered a completely non-exhaustive list of intriguing and entertaining words across twelve different European languages, for which there is no easy English equivalent.

These words are like the 'Big 5' of language learning. These are the elephants, the buffalos, the lions and the cheetahs that you'll come across when learning a new language. But, of course, the joy of going on a once-in-a-lifetime safari trip is not just in seeing those animals up close that you recognise from the picture books. You equally enjoy the scenery, the sunsets, eating by the campfire, and the stars as you look up into the night sky. An immense amount of pleasure and interest can be gathered from the more ordinary parts of learning another language too. There is no greater satisfaction than being able to make yourself understood to someone from a different country. There is no moment more memorable than that first time you make a joke in a foreign language that makes someone laugh.

With the right motivation, suitable expectations and access to the necessary resources, anybody can learn another language at any point in their lives. The aim of this book is to offer an amusing glimpse into the magical world of discovery and the treasures that await those who do.

French

The UK is separated from France by just a thin stretch of shallow water, which we proudly call the English Channel. The French nonchalantly call it *La Manche*, or 'the Sleeve'. At its narrowest point, the Sleeve is only 150ft (45m) deep and only 20 miles (32km) wide, which reminds us just how close to the continent our island is. We call that part the Dover Strait, and the French call it *Le Pas-de-Calais*, or the 'Calais Strait'.

Despite the fact that, seemingly, neither side can agree on what to call anything, the histories of the UK and France could hardly be more closely intertwined. For many, the history of modern Britain began when a Frenchman named William the Conqueror (the French call him William II) crossed the Calais Strait in 1066 and – as his name might suggest – quickly conquered the country. He found a land full of people speaking a mixture of Saxon German and Celtic Welsh, and so introduced Norman French into the equation. From this mix, the language we speak today was born: a broadly Germanic structure with heavy influence from Celtic languages and almost half of its words borrowed from French, which we call English.

The English might have been quite happy to throw open their arms to French words that sounded fancier than their existing Germanic stock (such as 'cordial reception' instead of 'hearty welcome') but it's perhaps fair to say that back on the continent our Gallic cousins have been less enthusiastic about reciprocating the gesture. Keeping English and other influences as far away as possible from the French language is even an activity that has given people their livelihoods for centuries. The infamous *Academie Française*, or 'French Academy', was established in the seventeenth century to try to keep French 'pure', which effectively meant to make sure that everyone else in France started talking like they did in Paris; in recent times it has been leading a ferocious effort to keep Anglicisms off the streets of France.

As an example, French radio stations used to be obliged to play a minimum number of songs in French in addition to English chart songs or risk being taken off the air. That particular law may have been dropped after heavy lobbying in 2016, but among many in France this protectionist and linguistically conservative attitude still remains. The French are as proud of their language as the British are of driving on the wrong side of the road. France's former president Jacques Chirac even made a point of storming out of summits, press conferences and interviews if journalists asked him questions in English, or even if someone just mentioned the

English language in a positive light, all to the tacit approval of the French public.

Yet for all its idiosyncrasies, French is a wonderful language. It is the language of gastronomy, of good wine, of music, of literature and, of course, of love. And as we're about to see, French is a versatile and attractive tongue that has masterfully captured many of life's intricate nuances.

///

DÉPAYSEMENT [noun]   /day-pay-z-MON/

Travelling the world is a wonderful thing. Nothing broadens your perspectives and challenges your preconceptions more than seeing how people live in other countries, noticing the differences and similarities between their lives and yours. However, on all long trips there comes a point where the exoticism of being in a foreign place might tip over into frustration. Why are there so many mosquitoes everywhere, and why does everyone look so alarmed they might call an ambulance every time you ask for a spot of milk in your tea?

The French understand the discomfort of being away from home very well, and as a result they have created the perfect word for it. It means homesickness, culture shock, disorientation and a longing to be back among familiar surroundings: *dépaysement*, which literally means 'de-country-ment', or the state of having been removed from where you are from.

FLÂNER [verb]   /flah-NAY/

One of the true pleasures, though, of going on holiday to a foreign country is the glorious art of doing nothing. You're not rushing to get to work, nobody needs to be picked up from school and you don't have a whole list of things you need to get from town before the shops close. So don't hurry, don't stress, just put on a pair of comfy shoes and go for a gentle stroll at a pace so comfortable that you almost feel like you're sitting down. Sit your eyes out on stalks and let them sweep the horizon, from left to right, up and down, absorbing every detail of every building that you pass, and soak in the atmosphere of the new place that you find yourself in.

In French, this is called *flâner*. This verb literally means just to wander at a relaxed pace through a city, soaking up the atmosphere. Next time you go to Paris remember there's no need to pay those extortionate entry fees to museums or queue for hours to go up the Eiffel Tower. Just wander through the quaint little streets and when you get back and people ask you what you did, just tell them that you *flâner*-ed about.

L'APPEL DU VIDE [noun]   /lap-PELL dyoo VEED/

If there's one thing that unites people all over the world, it's this. No matter where you go, from Portugal to Bosnia, from Thailand to Chile, you will find people who climb up on to very high surfaces and jump. In places like Porto and Mostar, you'll find it's teenagers who climb up on bridges and send their friends to go around asking incredulous tourists to first make a donation before they plunge into the fast-moving river below. In other places, you might find it's tourists themselves who'll happily strap themselves to elasticated ropes and throw themselves into the ravine, with blind faith that the rope will hold them. And if that's not enough, you can even pay someone to take you up several thousand feet into the air on an aeroplane and then leap out, triggering your parachute whenever you're ready.

Why are we so entranced by this peculiar dance with death? Whatever the reason, the truth is that many of us have a gnawing curiosity about what it would be like to plunge through hundreds of metres of atmosphere and live to tell the tale. The French have a nice term to explain this urge: *l'appel du vide*, which literally means 'the call of the void'.

///

EMPÊCHEMENT [noun]   /om-pesh-MON/

The French essentially invented modern-day social life. France's cities are filled with millions of cafés, brasseries, bistros and restaurants with chequered multicoloured chairs and shiny marble-topped tables. Local people can spend their entire weekends flitting in between these cafés from social engagement to social engagement, drinking a coffee here, a glass of wine there, smoking the odd cigarette under a heater in the winter or reading a couple of pages of whatever book they have to hand.

Every now and then, though, their plans might be interrupted. Suddenly they might find themselves unable to make an engagement with someone that they'd arranged weeks before, because at the last minute something has come up. Maybe a pipe has burst at home, the car won't start, the trains are on strike, they've had an invitation from someone they'd prefer to see instead. Or maybe they just decided that they'd rather spend the day reclined on the couch, reflecting on the meaning of life while gazing through their French windows at passers-by in the street below. Whatever it is, that thing in French is called an *empêchement* and is a perfectly reasonable way to cancel on someone at the last minute. It literally means a 'prevention'.

RETROUVAILLES [noun]   /ruh-troov-EYE/

The world is getting smaller, but we're finding more opportunities than ever before to spend more time in different parts of it. Young people, unimpressed by the thought of going straight into working nine to six every day with twenty days' leave per year, are tending to just pack a rucksack, book a flight somewhere and go off travelling for a few months or years until they've worked out what they want to do. People in their late 20s, early 30s and older are coming to the conclusion that life in their home countries isn't all it's cracked up to be and are finding there are better chances overseas in places where they might one day actually to be able to afford to buy a house. Pensioners are spending their whole lives saving for that day when they can book a one-way ticket to somewhere sunnier and spend their days reading by the pool and soaking up the vitamin D they've always lacked. All of this is like a dream come true for the individual concerned, but inevitably they will carry guilt about those that they've left behind. Even with all the technology in the world, when you move away from your friends, family and loved ones to pursue a life overseas, a distance develops between you that becomes increasingly hard to bridge.

Yet it's all worth it for that truly magical moment when you see each other again. Those reunions at airports, railway stations or wherever you meet that person again after so long are really special. They make the months or years of heartache that precede them disappear. The French language recognises that these are no ordinary meetings. They are bursting with emotion and joy. They are *retrouvailles*.

PARLER YAOURT [verb] /par-LAY ya-OOR/

It will come as no surprise to anyone from the UK that we don't exactly have a reputation around the world for being particularly proactive about speaking foreign languages. Many of us have mastered the art of smile-and-point, or can manage impeccably to slow down the pace of our English so that people around the world can understand us. But when it comes to actually speaking the languages, we trail in the wake of our European neighbours such as Sweden, the Netherlands, Greece and Portugal, all of which have populations where more than 50 per cent of people can hold a conversation in at least one other language.

Fortunately, though, we're not alone. The French are slightly better than us, but not by much. Instead of Britain's trademark smile-and-point technique, the French have developed a rather marvellous tactic that they deploy to get by wherever they are in the world. *Parler yaourt*, which literally means 'to speak yoghurt', is when you speak another language incredibly badly with lots of mistakes, making up lots of words as you go along, or just saying French words in what sounds like a convincing accent. You can also *chanter yaourt*, or 'sing yoghurt', when you try to sing along to a song you don't know the words to.

RÂLER [verb]   /rah-LAY/

France has bestowed upon the world many great things. Exquisite wines, unbeatable cheeses, world-class gastronomy and lots of existentialist philosophy. The last of these things – existentialism – is a defining feature of modern French life. Those brasseries across Paris will be full of people sipping bitter coffees, loosening their ties and letting off steam to their friends about everything that is wrong or imperfect in life. Why do the shops have to close on a Sunday? Why is the price of rent so high? Why is the government putting up even more taxes or threatening to raise the retirement age by six months?

The French have taken what we know as having a bit of a moan and turned it into an art. The French can complain about the world more beautifully and more persuasively than almost any other country on Earth. As this developed, the word 'complain' no longer held any gravitas in the face of this magnificent onslaught of doubts. The French language therefore provided a new word that fit it much better: *râler*, 'to let off steam and criticise the world'.

CARTONNER [verb]   /car-tonn-AY/

Sometimes things are so successful that they take the world by storm. In France, the hazelnut chocolate spread known as Nutella (which, incidentally, is Italian) has become such an integral part of French life that in January 2018 there were riots in one of France's leading supermarkets because it was offering an exceptionally generous discount on large tubs of it, which led customers to fight each other in the queues to get their hands on it.

That might remind you of the similarly rather ugly scenes on Oxford Street in 2007 when Primark's first superstore opened and shoppers broke the all holy British tradition of orderly queuing by punching each other to be the first in line to get all the best deals.

These brands are real successes, and French rewards such successes with a special verb: *cartonner*. This means 'to cardboard' and refers to when you hit the cardboard target square on at a shooting range. If we were to translate this idiomatically, perhaps in English we'd say: 'to bullseye'.

JE NE SAIS QUOI [noun]   /zhuh nuh say KWAH/

Our experience of the world is inherently limited by our ability to express our thoughts, feelings and reactions with language. All languages are inherently limited, as they tend to capture the experience of a certain group of people or culture in the world. That, of course, is fine, because we can invent new words and see if they catch on, or borrow words from other languages that seem to make sense.

The French language, to its credit, at least recognises its own limitations. When French speakers reach that abyss of running out of words to express why they like something, they can stealthily dodge the more pernickety questions that arise by simply saying that they like it because it has a certain *je ne sais quoi*, or 'I don't know what'. *Je ne sais quoi* is a pretty versatile expression and can be used to describe anything that we like or find attractive, but just can't quite explain why. *Je ne sais quoi* is the linguistic equivalent of shrugging your shoulders, smiling sweetly and standing your ground.

SAVOIR FAIRE [noun]   /sa-vwar FAIR/

Some people have extraordinary talents for certain things. They can be an extremely gifted dancer, musician, businessman, computer programmer, interpreter and so on. But talent only gets you so far. It's great to be talented at any of those things, but if you don't work on it and become skilled at it, then it's hard for you to really reap the benefits of whatever it is that you're naturally good at.

The French word *savoir faire*, which literally means 'to know to do', refers to more than just talent. It's the combination of talent with skill and technique, all to an extraordinarily high degree. Someone's *savoir faire* is their unique and special art, their way of doing things that makes them exceptionally good at it, and is something for us mere mortals to aspire to achieving.

///

CRISE DE FOIE [noun]   /creez duh FWAH/

France is famous for having some of the best gastronomy in the world. French cuisine is celebrated in so many countries, and French cooking techniques have influenced world-class chefs everywhere. As you might imagine for a country with such a legacy, food is an important part of French culture, and in particular there is a really high appreciation of good-quality cooking.

The inevitable consequence of that is that for those of us who really enjoy our food, to the point where we just don't want to stop eating, we can get in some rather uncomfortable situations. For hours after a meal we might be moaning and clutching our stomachs, regretting everything but knowing that in a few hours we're going to repeat it all again. In English we know this as 'indigestion', but in French it's a rather more alarming affair. A *crise de foie* is a 'liver attack' and is the French way of understanding when your body's telling you that you're having too much of a good thing.

SE DÉBROUILLER [verb]   /suh day-broo-wee-YAY/

When life presents us with setbacks, our first instinct might be to reach for the phone and call someone to ask for their help. But if that specific setback is that your phone has inexplicably run out of all of its battery just minutes after you've taken it off the charge, you might find yourself a little bit stuck. Not only are you unable to call anyone, but you can't even look for help on the internet either, as your one little life source has decided to pack things in and leave you for the time being to your own devices.

When you're in that situation and you're faced with a dilemma you need to solve and manage to work things out without any help or guidance from anyone else, the French reward you with your own verb: *se débrouiller*. This literally means 'to de-fog yourself', or shake off the shrouds of uncertainty that you must have been stuck in when you first tried to fix things, but that dissipated when you finally got the thing to turn on again. *Se débrouiller*: when you work things out for yourself.

BRICOLEUR [noun]   /bree-koh-LUHR/

A good workman never blames his tools, but unfortunately there are a lot of bad workmen out there. We all know the type who will turn up, after you patiently explain the problem in great detail over the phone, only to tell you that he can't fix it today because he has to go back and get more equipment. He'll have to come back another day and charge you another £50 call-out fee.

A good handyman, however, will try and fix the problem come what may and with whatever tools they happen to have available. In French, those can-do handymen who will always fix the problem no matter what have got their own name: *bricoleur.*

MATRAQUAGE FISCAL [noun]   /mah-trah-KAJ fee-SKALL/

France has a long tradition of electing politicians, liking them for five minutes and then feeling so incensed by whatever it is they try to do that they shut down all the schools, blockade the ports and take to the streets for weeks and months to make sure that someone, somewhere is aware of the fact that they're not happy. This rather admirable spirit of revolution is what makes France the wonderful place it is today, and in periods of crisis it has often been eyed with some envy by those of us across the other side of the Sleeve.

One of the most sensitive topics in France is taxation. In 2013, French actor and national treasure Gerard Depardieu was so horrified to discover that President François Hollande was planning to impose a 75 per cent levy on his higher income that he immediately called the Kremlin in Moscow and asked for Russian citizenship. This kind of tax policy in French is called *matraquage fiscal,* or 'fiscal bludgeoning', and is when people feel bludgeoned by the amount of tax that they are being asked to pay.

FRAPPADINGUE [noun]   /frah-pah-DANG/

When you live in a country that every now and then will fiscally bludgeon you without a second thought, and where you can't move for people *râler*-ing about how awful life is, it's not a surprise that every now and then you might lose your temper and fly into a little bit of a rage. 'A little bit of a rage' is, of course, a perfect example of British euphemism, for what we really mean by that kind of thing is what the French call *frappadingue*. *Frappadingue* is when you are so angry and so crazy that you roam around like a lunatic, as if delirious from someone hitting you over the head.

ÊTRE SORTABLE / ÊTRE INSORTABLE [verb]   /EH-truh sor-TAH-bluh/ /EH-truh an-sor-TAH-bluh/

If you have any relatives who are *frappadingue*, then they will be totally *insortable*. When your eccentric aunt and uncle call you up because they're in town and would like to take you out for a meal somewhere nice that you know, you might start to panic. Your eccentric aunt and uncle are classic examples of being *insortable*. They wear weird jumpers, they complain to the staff at your favourite restaurant that the food wasn't really good enough, they ask you embarrassing and piercing personal questions about how your life is going – and worst of all, they might lean over and tap the person on the next table to tell them that they have a bit of food around their mouth. Do not *sortir* with those particular relatives, for they are *insortable*.

But then you might have relatives who are *sortable*. They dress normally, they're polite, they don't complain and they certainly don't do anything that makes you wish the ground would swallow you up there and then where you're sitting. The great thing, however, is that in French it's possible to distinguish between these very distinct kinds of relatives. There are relatives that you wouldn't mind being seen in public with, and those relatives are *sortable*, from the verb *sortir*, which means 'to go out'. And there are those who are so *insortable* that when they invite you out you will sit and pray for any kind of *empêchement* to avoid the experience.

JOLIE LAIDE [adjective]   /zhoh-LEE led/

'Beauty is in the eye of the beholder'. For centuries, we have mistakenly thought that this rather wonderful sentiment of Shakespeare's was a fairly British invention and one of the many things we had given to the world. However, the French language strongly contradicts this and even goes one step further by having a word that crystallises this in everyday language. It recognises the fact that beauty is extremely subjective, and that it is no coincidence that in fact some of the most beautiful people in the world do not, by most accounts, conform to the conventional ideals of beauty that we see on Instagram.

The word *jolie laide* literally means 'pretty-ugly' (not 'pretty ugly', that would be *assez laide*). It means that someone can both be pretty and ugly at the same time, but mainly refers to the idea that someone is beautiful precisely because they are unconventional looking.

//

LA DOULEUR EXQUISE [noun]   /la doo-LUHR ex-KEEZ/

Paris is known as the city of love, and France in general is a place that is very in touch with its romantic side. People fall in love, they have brief affairs, they get married, they divorce, they live together forever, they date, and there is an extremely casual attitude towards all of these things, as well as several hundred years of literature, art, poetry and film that have tried to discover all of the truths around the mind-bogglingly complicated topic of love.

Yet perhaps one of the most tragic and soul-destroying feelings that one can ever experience in life is to love someone who does not love you back. Unrequited love, in its injustice, its intangibility and its defeatism, is not seen necessarily as something so negative in French. The French language recognises the pain and heartbreak that it causes, but it also suggests that those feelings are some of the most beautiful and most exquisite that are available to the human experience. Hence the French expression *la douleur exquise*, 'the exquisite pain' of unrequited love.

AMOURETTE [noun]   /ah-moo-RETT-uh/

In French, you can have an *amour*. This is a long love affair, a relationship that lasts many years and becomes a defining feature of your life. But not all such relationships are supposed to last forever. Sometimes, they're much shorter. They can be little flings that last just for a summer, a few months or a few weeks. Those things are not *amours*, they're just little flames that light up and then extinguish themselves fairly soon after. In French that is called an *amourette*, a 'little love'. Sure, it's not going to last forever, but it's a nice little thing to be able to smile about on the Métro in the mornings.

★

Spanish

Spanish is the world's second most commonly spoken language. More people speak Spanish than English as a native language. The only other language that more people speak is Mandarin Chinese. Spanish is the official language of much of South and Central America, and is nowadays widely spoken in the USA and Canada as well. And just think, Spanish all started in a little place in Europe called Spain, and in particular in an area called Castile.

Spanish is often called Castilian, or *castellano*, as a reminder of the fact that it is not the only language of Spain. Spain is a multilingual country, with other languages like Basque, Galician and Catalan spoken in different parts of it. What we now call Spanish originally came from the north of Spain and was standardised over the course of a few centuries in Toledo. It was then adopted by Madrid and gradually spread to become the common language across the whole of Spain, and eventually of Latin America as well.

Spanish is a very beautiful language and is one of the most popular that people start learning as adults. Many things make learning Spanish more straightforward than other languages such as neighbouring French, for example. Spanish is written very phonetically, which means that once you've understood the logic of the writing system, you're very unlikely to mispronounce anything. There are also many words in Spanish that are very similar to English, such as *diferencia* or 'difference', *opción* or 'option', and *frecuencia* or 'frequency'.

One big difference between Spanish and English, though, is the two languages' different perceptions of word efficiency. In English, our words tend to be short and to the point. Many words consist of just one syllable, and we stick words together in a fashion that seems logical and concise. In Spanish, however, words can be much longer, and some things that are just one word in English can be a whole phrase in Spanish. For example, a 'credit card' in English is a *tarjeta de crédito* in Spanish, or literally a 'card of credit'. 'Tourist information' is '*la oficina de información turística*', or 'the office of touristic information'.

People in Spain are known for their passion and their expressiveness, and so it should come as no surprise that that is reflected in their language. The Spanish range of vocabulary for emotions in particular is truly impressive. It'd be interesting to see what introducing a whole set of vocabulary like that into English might unlock in the British psyche ...

DUENDE [noun]   /DWEN-deh/

Spain is a pretty spectacular place. It is surrounded almost on all sides by the sea, with magnificent coastlines to the north and white sandy beaches along the east. In the centre, it is made up of great plains and breathtaking mountain ranges that in the south drop straight down into the sea. Spain is the kind of place where you can hardly turn a corner without gasping out of awe for the natural beauty that it exhibits – and it is precisely that sense of awe in the face of the truly sublime that the word *duende* means.

Duende is not just something that you experience from nature, however. The concept of *duende* also comes from the entrancing moves and song of the Flamenco performers, who for centuries have been dancing and singing across all the little bars of Spain, moving their audiences with their stunning combination of raw emotion and technique.

Duende is present whenever you have that jaw-dropping sense of admiration for something in life that is so spellbinding and wonderful it produces a physical and emotional reaction.

ATURDIR [verb]   /ah-toor-DEER/

Not too far removed from *duende* is the Spanish verb *aturdir*. There are many things that can have this effect on you. Perhaps you went round to your friend's house and were so shocked by how ugly her new wallpaper was that your mind went completely blank. Or perhaps someone just told you some really unexpected and big news in their life and you are stunned to silence.

For something to *aturdir* you, it can be good or bad. Essentially, the main idea here is that you're so overwhelmed, stunned or bewildered by something that not only can you not speak, but actually your entire mind goes blank. Your brain simply cannot process the information that you are passing on to it, and so it simply shuts down.

EMPALAGAR [verb]   /em-pah-lah-GAR/

We all love sweet things: chocolate, custard, ice cream, cakes, sticky buns, anything with a layer of icing on it. We love sweet things so much that we even have entire festivals dedicated to eating them, like Easter when we traditionally eat so much chocolate that we practically burst. However, the problem really is that we don't always know when we should stop. Or at least, we may have an idea of when we should have stopped, but by that point it's normally too late.

Part of the reason for this is that in English we don't have a word to describe that particular feeling of something being so sweet that it'll make you feel sick. As a result, we can't warn people that they should be careful about, for example, sitting down to eat an entire multipack of Kinder Buenos themselves, because it will almost certainly have that effect on them. Therefore, sadly, that knowledge of what will and won't be so sweet it'll make you sick is frequently lost in the English language. Hence the need for the Spanish verb *empalagar*, which we should perhaps be putting on warning labels on certain types of food. It means 'to be so sweet it will make you sick'.

SOBREMESA [noun]   /soh-breh-MEH-sah/

In restaurants in the UK, no sooner have your knife and fork touched your empty plate than your waiter will be back, lifting your plate away from your table and asking you with a pointed smile whether you'd like to spend more money on a dessert or coffee, or whether you want to just get it all over and done with and have the bill now. In many parts of the UK, it might even be a good idea to start reaching for your credit card as soon as you feel like you might be down to your last few bites of whatever you're eating, just so you can pay and get out of the restaurant as quickly as possible and leave your table vacant for the next customers.

This custom is a total anathema to everything that Spanish culture stands for. In Spain, chasing someone out of a restaurant because they've finished their food is an offence of almost criminal proportions. For in Spain the entire meal is simply an entrée. As forks get put down and people start digesting, so commences the most important part of the evening meal: the *sobremesa*. This is when people kick back, pour themselves another drink, open their hearts and start talking to one another long into the balmy night, perhaps sitting out on a quaint square somewhere under the stars. Nobody is rushing to kick you out and nobody is in a hurry to leave either. The *sobremesa* is when all the most important conversations of the day happen, and nobody is going to rush that.

///

PISCOLABIS [noun]   /piss-coh-LAB-iss/

In the UK we tend to eat between once and twice per day. We'll shovel down some cereal in the morning while simultaneously brushing our teeth, tying our shoelaces, washing our hair and running for the train. Then in the evening we might boil some pasta when we get back, to which the more daring of us might add something like tinned tuna and cheese, which we'll eat without once looking down at our plates as our eyes are glued to the TV. At work, it is generally frowned upon to do anything except sit at your desk and type mechanically into your computer. It is not usually allowed to get up for any reason, least of all to eat. If you're lucky, you might persuade someone to bring you a bacon sandwich from a nearby petrol station, which you can eat with one hand as you keep trying to type with the other, raining a shower of crumbs that penetrate the sinister gaps between the keys of your keyboard.

In Spain, things are very different. Your lunch break may be as long as the working day itself, and if you're still hungry there are plenty of opportunities to get up and make yourself a drink and have a snack. These mid-work snacks are such an important part of life that they even have a name in Spanish: *piscolabis*.

ENCHILADO [adjective]   /en-chill-AH-doh/

Around the world, the UK has a rather unfair reputation for liking rather bland foods. This may be because for centuries, all we ate was roasted meat with boiled root vegetables. Nevertheless, things have changed now and we have a much more varied diet made up of many different foods from all over the world. Nowadays, one of our favourite foods is Indian, and as a result many of us like to think that we're actually quite good at handling spice.

That is, of course, until you go to somewhere like Mexico, the largest Spanish-speaking country in the world, where you really begin to understand what spice means. In Mexico, people eat mouth-scorchingly hot chilli peppers just for fun and even hold competitions to see who can eat the most. As a result, they came up with an ingenious word to describe that state of torturous burning that you subject the inside of your mouth to when you eat too many chillies: *enchilado*.

HUEVÓN [noun]   /we-BON/

Bureaucracy is something of a myth in the English language. We are in the awful habit of calling something bureaucratic or cumbersome because we had to fill in an online form that had a maximum of three questions, all of which were yes/no tick boxes. We then hit send, tut, complain about how long that took, and then a few days later whatever we wanted to happen, happens.

In the Spanish-speaking world, bureaucracy is a word that strikes terror into the heart of anyone who speaks the language. Memories will come flooding back of having to set up camp outside government offices throughout the night just in order to be in the queue for hours to renew your passport or tax documents, only to be told that you'd filled in one of the sections on the fifty-nine-page form wrong and would have to go away and return just before sunrise again the next day. And at the heart of all this are the people who process it all with about as much enthusiasm as a Persian cat in the rain. Those people who hate their jobs, are no good at them, think they have a divine right to have them and probably got there because of some kind of dodgy connection anyway, have a name in Spanish: *huevón*, which literally means 'a massive egg'.

LAMPIÑO [noun]   /lam-PEE-nyoh/

The arrival of hipsters was like manna from heaven for many Spanish men. After years of having to grapple with razors, foam and shaving brushes several times a day to maintain their appearance, finally they could let loose and grow their beards out to their hearts' content and even look cool in the process. Stereotypically, in Spain facial hair is as widespread as oranges, so much so that the Spanish language even has a word to describe those very rare specimens of men who, unfortunately, are not blessed with the gift of being able to grow a beard.

Those men whose faces are as smooth in their late 40s as they were in their early teens are called *lampiños*. Perhaps we especially need this word in English, as the hipster beard craze has revealed the fact that a large proportion of the world's *lampiños* – this author included – seem to have roots in the UK.

PAVONEARSE [verb]   /pah-boh-neh-AR-seh/

If you've got it, though, flaunt it. In English we might strut around like peacocks when we want to show off about something, but in Spanish people who show off might remind you of a slightly different animal. Those people who see the handrail on a packed Tube carriage as the perfect opportunity for them to start doing their morning pull-ups, or who buy the flashiest car imaginable just to let everyone else in the supermarket car park know that they're actually quite successful, in Spanish are nowhere near as glamorous as peacocks. In Spanish those people are compared to the pink-neck-wobbling, noisy, gobbling yet beautiful creatures that are turkeys. Those people *pavonearse*, which means 'to turkey about'.

ENTRECEJO [noun]   /en-treh-THE-khoh/

Perhaps one of the flipsides of being blessed with perfect facial hair from about the age of 11 is that you don't always have control over all the other places in which your hair might also start growing. The concept of a 'monobrow' is nothing new to the English language. We've known about that for years and have a perfectly good word for it. In Spanish, however, not only do they have the word for a monobrow, but they also have a word for the exact opposite: *entrecejo*. This is a complete conceptual gap in the English language. What on Earth do we call the space between your eyebrows? Even if there's a fancy medical term, we certainly don't have a word that we use in everyday life. As a result, here come the Spanish to our rescue with *entrecejo*.

MANCO [noun] /MAN-koh/

In a similarly perceptive vein, one of Spanish's real assets is the fact that it has so many simple words that mean things that in English we are forced to try to clunkily describe in long-winded and awkward noun phrases that none of us really know whether we should be inserting hyphens into or not. For example, if somebody has one arm, would you refer to them as a 'one armed man' or a 'one-armed man' or simply 'someone who has one arm'? The Spanish, with their precise and thorough lexicon, are utterly bemused by this dilemma, for in this case they would simply say the word *manco*.

TUERTO [noun] /TWER-toh/

Leaving the problem of people who have one arm to one side, what on Earth do you do if someone only has one eye? To hyphenate, not to hyphenate, or simply to describe in as broad and imprecise terms as possible? Once again, Spanish beats the English language hands down in this case with the word *tuerto*, which means 'somebody who has only one eye'.

///

LIGÓN [noun]   /lee-GON/

Since the advent of modern technology, going on a date with someone you may or may not be romantically interested in is now only as complicated as a swipe on your smartphone. As a result, dating culture has exploded in the UK. Once seen as something that only happened in American sitcoms, now people go on dates all the time and even spend the rare evenings that they're not going on dates at home, watching TV programmes about other people's first awkward romantic encounters. For some people, though, what might otherwise be a fairly under-control national obsession can tip over into being something a little bit more problematic.

When someone just can't stop going on dates with different people, and even flirting with the restaurant staff while they're on those dates or trying to get the person on the next table's number, be wary. In Spanish, they're clearly marked and labelled so everybody knows that they are bad news, with the word *ligón*. This comes from the verb *ligar* which means 'to connect' or 'hook up', which is combined with that wonderful Spanish suffix -*ón*, which always means 'a big one'.

MIMOSO [noun]   /mee-MOH-soh/

Maybe it's just our colder climate. Maybe it's our world-famous reluctance to show our emotions to others. Or maybe it's a mixture of both of those two things and some other complexities too, but whatever the reason, for as long as anyone can remember British people have been famed for being awkward about physical contact. What do you do when you meet someone? Do you shake their hand, do you kiss their cheek, do you keep your hands firmly in your pockets and nod very non-committally? Maybe you should go in for a bear hug? Because we don't have any rules about this, the vast majority of first-time encounters in British culture are quite awkward and made better only by the fact that you can only meet someone for the first time once.

Needless to say, things are again quite different in the Spanish world, where people kiss each other on the cheek, embrace, clasp each other's hands, slap each other on the back and generally have no problem with physical contact at all. In fact, there are even some people who really enjoy hugs, kisses, cuddles, handshakes and any other kind of affection in that way. Those people are called *mimosos*, which is so un-British a concept that perhaps we should just about consider embracing it. Not too strongly, though.

VERGÜENZA AJENA [noun]   /ber-GWEN-thah ah-KHEH-nah/

You know those times when you see somebody totally unaware suffering the most horrendous wardrobe malfunction imaginable and you just die a little bit inside on their behalf? Or perhaps you see someone on a date with someone who's clearly a *ligón* and there's no chemistry between them and you find you can barely watch for fear of not having a large enough hole nearby for you to jump in and be swallowed by the Earth?

In Spanish, that feeling is extremely well known and experienced by many different people. So much so, in fact, that it even has its own name: *vergüenza ajena*. This means 'embarrassment on others' behalf' and is experienced when you see someone doing something that makes you cringe so much you almost feel as though you are experiencing all of their shame for them.

ENMADRARSE [verb]   /en-mah-DRAR-seh/

Family is extremely important in Spanish culture. People don't just make an effort to see their parents and siblings, but they also go out for huge meals and celebrate special occasions with all their cousins, aunts, uncles, grandparents, second cousins, nephews and nieces too. By far the most important figure of all in the family, though, is the mother, who occupies a very special place in Spanish life. Award-winning Spanish director Pedro Almodóvar regularly talks about the impact his mother had on him and on his work, and even produced an entire film called *Todo sobre mi madre*, or *All About My Mother*. The word *enmadrarse*, therefore, is a very important one for which we simply don't have an equivalent in English.

Enmadrarse is when a child is very emotionally attached to his or her mother. When the mother's not there, the world ends for that child, who simply always wants to be by her side.

MADRUGAR [verb]   /mah-droo-GAR/

There was a time when Spain and the UK were in the same time zone. Both countries used GMT, which meant that when it was midday in London, it was also midday in Madrid. This made quite a lot of sense, because most of Spain is in fact much further west than the UK. Incidentally, at this time France too used the same time zone as the UK, forming a nice little block of Western European countries that you didn't have to change your watch when you travelled to. But then came the Second World War, and France's German occupiers forced them to move their clocks one hour forward so that they would be on the same time as Berlin. Spain was ruled at that point by the military dictator Franco, who was sympathetic to the Germans and decided to also move Spain's time zone one hour forward to what is now known as Central European Time. After the war was over, neither Spain nor France ever bothered to change their clocks back, meaning that nowadays whenever Brits travel anywhere in Europe (apart from Portugal or Ireland), we keep having to change our watches back and forth.

As a result, the sun rises extremely late in Spain, at around 7 a.m. in midsummer and closer to 9 a.m. in midwinter, which means that the concept of getting up at the crack of dawn is not quite as impressive as in some other places. Yet, nonetheless,

Spanish has a great word for when you do get up at the same time as the sun: *madrugar*.

RECOGERSE [verb]   /reh-koh-KHER-seh/

The idea of living in Spain is a dream come true for many Brits. In fact, around a million of us have sold up in the UK and moved out to the Iberian Peninsula to live our days in the warmth and sunshine of the Mediterranean coast. This is evident if you look at a satellite image of certain parts of Spain and see the many hundreds of houses equipped with nice swimming pools, all armed with enormous satellites that beam Sky Sports into British expats' living rooms.

However, those who don't watch British TV all day might instead spend their afternoons outside, on their verandas in the shade with a good book, enjoying the heat and watching the sun make its way across the mountainside. When the sun disappears and the temperatures recede, that's the point at which they might *recogerse*. This fantastic Spanish word means to move back inside in the evening after a long day outside in the warm weather.

PUENTE [noun]   /PWEN-teh/

With the exception of Christmas and New Year, in the UK all of our national holidays are on a Monday. At first glance, this seems like a great idea because you always get a long weekend, which you can spend crammed into a low-cost airline seat, trying to get somewhere with nicer weather. In other parts of the world, though, national holidays can be on any day of the week, depending on whichever date it is that is of national significance. This may seem annoying if the holiday falls on a Thursday, as you'd imagine that you can't make a long weekend of it, but when that happens the Spanish have come up with an ingenious concept which knocks the UK's Monday bank holidays well into the long grass. *Puente*, meaning 'bridge', is the day between two national holidays, or a national holiday and a weekend, which you can feel free to take off as well, so that instead of a three-day weekend you get a four-day weekend, or even more. At this point you might wonder when a long weekend stops being a long weekend and starts being a week, but that is most definitely against the spirit of *puente*.

BOTELLÓN [noun]   /boh-teh-YON/

For many of us, the idea of drinking in a park is quite unappealing once you're old enough to be able to sit in a pub. In Spain, though, drinking outside is a way of life. Especially in the warmer months, it's possible to sit outside long into the warm evenings without even the slightest thought of having to prevent frostbite. As a result, many people gather in large groups with their friends and jugs and bottles and cans of anything they fancy and have a good time. In Spanish this is called a *botellón*, which means a large open-air drinking party in a public space, like in a park or on a beach.

FRIOLERO [noun] /free-oh-LEH-roh/

It's very easy to spot Spanish people in the UK, because on those rare days in July when the temperature rises above 19 degrees and the clouds break to allow about forty-five minutes of sunshine to pass through and everyone strips down to as little outer clothing as legally possible and rushes to find a spot in the nearest park, Spanish people are still wearing coats and gloves and scarves. You can also spot them by the sound of their teeth chattering as they wait at bus stops. You can imagine that anyone used to temperatures regularly rising over 40 degrees Celsius in the summer would be extremely sensitive to the cold. In Spanish, those people who shriek and reach for a woolly hat at the slightest hint of a cool breeze are called *frioleros*.

CALUROSO [noun] /kah-loo-ROSS-oh/

At the opposite extreme are those who start sweating and feeling uncomfortable as soon as the temperatures hit double digits; many of us in the Uk would no doubt fall into this group! And Spanish has a word for those people too: *calurosos*.

TENER MANO IZQUIERDA [phrase] /teh-NER MAH-noh ith-KYER-thah/

Sometimes people are stubborn. You desperately need them to do something, but they just flat out refuse because they don't want to, or it's not in their interest. But some people in life have an extremely rare but powerful gift, which is the ability to persuade those they are negotiating with to do something, even though they don't want to do it or they know it's not in their interest.

Those people can skilfully manipulate a conversation, they know exactly when to apply the right amounts of pressure and sympathy in order to win over the other person, and in Spanish they rightfully earn themselves a whole expression to themselves: *tener mano izquierda*, which literally means 'to have a left hand'.

CACHARREAR [verb]   /cah-chah-rreh-AR/

Nowadays we live our whole lives surrounded by machines. Most of the time that's a great thing. It makes our lives far more convenient and far easier than they ever used to be. However, the problem is that sometimes things can go wrong, and for some reason a machine can stop working. The sensible thing to do in this case is to call in an expert, who can take a real look at the thing and find a way to fix it. However, some of us – particularly men – may be loath to do that, as we might feel that it in some way reflects badly on our virility. Therefore, to the groans of everyone else in the family, we'll try to fix everything ourselves, despite having next to zero technical knowledge and no idea how the machine works in the first place. This phenomenon, which has caused the early death of many a great machine, in Spanish is known as *cacharrear*.

Portuguese

Portugal grew up with two neighbours. On the one side it was surrounded by Spain, and on the other it had the vast expanse of the Atlantic Ocean and the world beyond. Faced with the two choices, Portugal quickly turned itself into one of the world's great seafaring nations and spread its language all over the Earth. Nowadays, Portuguese is the sixth most commonly spoken language in the world, which means that Portuguese is about a lot more than just Portugal. In fact, nowadays only 5 per cent of the world's Portuguese speakers actually live in Portugal.

Two hundred million people speak Portuguese in Brazil. It is the official language of six countries in Africa and still retains official status in the Chinese autonomous territory of Macau, right next to Hong Kong.

Brazilian Portuguese sounds markedly different to its European sibling, and there have been many differences and points of contention between the two sides. The two countries used to write totally differently until they both signed an orthographic agreement in 1990, after which they start spelling words the same way.

Nowadays, the relationship is a little bit like that of British and American English. Because Brazil produces the vast majority of the world's media in Portuguese, many in Portugal grow up watching and listening to Brazilian TV. They're comfortable with the Brazilian accent and can follow much of the local slang that has been introduced. People in Brazil, however, often claim not to be able to understand European Portuguese at all, as they have little exposure to it.

Due to its history, Portuguese has always been influenced by many different languages. During the time of the Moorish rule of Iberia, Portuguese adopted many Arabic words that are common parlance today, like *almofada*, which means 'pillow'. However, Portuguese has also had its influence on other languages, and in particular English. The English word 'to embarrass', for example, comes from the Portuguese *embaraçar*, as does the word 'fetish', which comes from the Portuguese *feitiço* and literally means a 'charm' or 'sorcery'.

Yet Portuguese's impressively global perspective could perhaps offer some more insights to other languages, as the following words might suggest.

///

SAUDADE [noun]   /sow-oo-DAH-gee/

In Lisbon, Portugal's cool and cosmopolitan capital, it's impossible to walk for more than a few hundred metres without discovering another breathtaking view and having to sit and enjoy it. Perhaps it's at precisely those moments when people feel *saudade*. Sitting on a bench, watching the sun creep back over to the other side of the world, watching the sea change colour, the buildings illuminate, the clouds shimmering, and suddenly you are beset by a feeling of incompleteness. It's a yearning, a melancholia for things that didn't happen. And why didn't they happen?

The beauty of *saudade* is in the fact that it's not an angry word. It's not about feeling hard done by or indignant. It's simply an acknowledgement that something didn't work out how you wanted it to and now you feel sad. So next time you feel down, ask yourself: is it *saudade*?

***

FUTEVÔLEI [noun]   /foo-chee-VOH-ley/

If there are two things that summon up that classic picture postcard image of life in Brazil better than anything else, it's football and beaches. Every year, millions of visitors flock to the white sandy beaches of Rio de Janeiro to enjoy that rare phenomenon of being both in a city and on a beach, and Brazil's national obsession with 'the beautiful game' is world famous by now.

This next word combines two of Brazil's passions and transforms them into something quite unique. If you're so confident of your football skills that you feel like you can happily play volleyball using just your feet, Brazil is the place for you. The game is called *futevôlei*, 'foot volley'.

CAFUNÉ [noun]   /kah-foo-NAY/

There's a reason why all the languages that derived from Latin are called 'Romance' languages, and Portuguese is no exception. This next word is for those tender moments that you spend with a loved one showing your affection by running your fingers gently through their hair. This is called *cafuné*.

LINDEZA [noun]   /lin-DEZ-ah/

One of Portuguese's greatest assets is its ability to identify grey areas of meaning between words in English and create the perfect words to fill them. The word *lindeza* is one of them. *Lindeza* means more than pretty, but less than beautiful. It means that you are young, attractive and stunning, but also approachable, amicable and jovial. In Portuguese, you can also describe things that have *lindeza* as *linda*, whether they are people, animals, views, houses, clothes, tastes, or anything really. You'll commonly hear people saying '*Que coisa mais linda!*' which means 'What a more [between-pretty-and-beautiful] thing!'

XODÓ [noun]   /choh-DOH/

You've been seeing someone for a while and really get on, you like each other and you're really happy with that state of affairs. You're at that stage in a relationship when you can just enjoy things and take them easy. There's no emotional baggage, no pressure, no mortgage and no expectation that you're going to start attending any distant in-laws' birthday parties. You're not quite officially boyfriend or girlfriend yet, but you're more than just friends.

Portuguese has the perfect word for that in-between stage. When people are not quite in a full-blown relationship yet, but are still taking things easy, they can call each other *xodó*.

AMORZÃO [noun]   /ah-mor-ZAONG/

When it's true love, you just know. You spend hours waiting for your phone to light up with a message from them, you count down the minutes until you can see each other again, you plan for months in advance all of the places you'd like to visit together, the countries you're going to move to, the colours you're going to paint the walls of your house, the pets, the kids ... There's nothing like meeting that one person you really click with. The one person you can really imagine spending the rest of your life with. The one person who's going to make you feel happy and safe forever.

In Portuguese, that person is not just your love. That person is your 'big love', and so you call them your *amorzão*. *Amor* means 'love', and *-ão* is something you can stick on the end of most words to mean 'really big'.

SÍTIO [noun]   /SEE-chuh/

People who love partying and socialising are drawn to living in a city like a magnet. But the irony is, without a penthouse flat or detached house with a garden, it's hard to throw truly epic parties while living in the city. The neighbours will complain, the police might get called and you'll forever be fretting about whether or not you're going to get your deposit back.

One solution to this is to get a place just outside of the city. Find somewhere where there are no neighbours to bother, there's a huge garden to spill out into and maybe there's a barbecue or a pool. There you can throw those enormous parties instead. In Portuguese, when you have a place like that you call it your *sítio*, which means 'location'.

SAIDEIRA [noun]   /sigh-DAY-ruh/

When you're out and begin to feel like it's time to start heading off, you might decide to have one last drink first. This will be the drink with which you bid goodbye to the night. In Portuguese, you call this your *saideira*. This literally means your 'departure drink' and comes from the word *saída* meaning 'exit' or 'departure'.

MALANDRO [noun]   /mal-AN-drooh/

Before you is an enigmatic figure, sitting at a small table in a café, probably reading some great work of philosophy, literature or political theory. When his friends arrive, he is fast-talking, sharp, witty and makes everyone laugh. He lives in the inner city, in some bohemian dwelling, probably with an unbeatable view of the city skyline, where he sits all day and ponders the meaning of life. He lives exactly the life that so many of us dream of, but with a twist.

This man's art is in his ability to project this image of himself as a bohemian, urbanite intellectual, but in fact you should take great care around him. His secret is that he is actually a great crook. Get too close and he'll take your money, pinch your car keys and write himself into your will. For this person is no ordinary man, he is a clever, witty, bohemian swindler. In Portuguese, he is a *malandro*.

///

MALEMOLÊNCIA [noun]   /mah-leh-mooh-LEHN-see-yuh/

One of the Portuguese language's greatest gifts to the world has been the gift of dance. Portuguese-speaking countries really can move, particularly of course in Brazil, where dancing is a way of life. Samba is one of the most famous forms of dance to have originated in Brazil and requires the dancer to be inhumanly flexible and supple in their movements. That ability to push your body into any shape necessary in order to match the music is called *malemolência*.

You can also use the word *malemolência* to refer to when you find yourself faced with a difficult problem there is no obvious way out of and so you resort to using creativity and lateral thinking to resolve it.

RECALQUE [noun]   /kheh-KAL-kee/

When a star shines too bright, it can attract a lot of attention. Yet some of the time, this is not always the attention that you'd want. When someone works hard to achieve something extraordinary, like finding a cure for a disease, or single-handedly launching an app that's going to revolutionise the way people live their lives, many people will be full of praise. Yet some people will turn green with envy and jealousy.

Some envious people will try to belittle your achievements, to make out like they're not as good as you think they are, or that the whole premise is in fact flawed. If they do it publicly, perhaps by writing a long and destructive opinion piece in a daily newspaper, or leaving a review trashing the whole thing online, then you're dealing with a very different beast. In Portuguese, that is called *recalque*.

FICANTE [noun]   /fee-KUHN-chee/

On the lower end of the relationship spectrum than a *xodó*, this word is for when you're not even at the stage where you can start to really see it as a relationship, but it's not just a one-off. This is 100 per cent no strings attached, but a regular fling. This is your *ficante*, which comes from the verb *ficar*, meaning 'to stay', and so can roughly be translated as something like your 'lingerer', or the person you keep going back to.

AZAR [noun]   /ah-ZAR/

Azar can strike at any moment. If you drop something and it breaks, that was *azar*. If you make it halfway down the stairs before realising you've forgotten your wallet, which then makes you miss the train, which then makes you late for work, which means you miss a meeting, which means you get fired, that was *azar* too. Anything bad or unjust that can happen to you in your daily life and that can deliver unwanted consequences all comes from one source: *azar*. And heaven help those unfortunate souls who 'are with *azar*', or *estar com azar*, and make sure you give them a wide berth.

REFOGAR [verb]   /khe-foh-GAR/

Portuguese speakers love their food. Portugal is home to some of the world's most exquisite fish dishes, sourced regularly from the enormous ocean that envelops them to the west, and for Brazilians eating out at a restaurant is a wholly different affair to what we're used to in the UK. Often food is laid out on huge banquet tables and you simply take a plate, help yourself to whatever you'd like in whatever quantities and then just pay by the weight, while also helping yourself to any of the roasted meat coming around, being cooked on terrifyingly sharp swords, known as *rodizio*.

Many dishes that are cooked in the Portuguese-speaking world start from a common place. The very first thing you do is heat up the pan, chop up an onion and then fry it gently in some heated oil before you start adding any other ingredients. This first step is such a staple that in the Portuguese language it has its own word: *refogar*.

CHATINHO / CHATÃO [noun]   /shah-CHEE-nyuh/ /shah-TAONG/

If someone annoys you, in Portuguese you can call them *chato*. This is a negative word that generally means some combination of boring, annoying, uninteresting and generally quite unlikeable. If that person who annoys you happens to also be quite short, you can call them a *chatinho*.

But before you get the impression that this is discriminatory to short people, if you're being annoyed by someone who is actually quite tall, you can instead call them a *chatão*. This is a useful tool in Portuguese, where you can add *-inho* to the end of anything to mean 'a small one', and *-ão* to the end of anything to mean 'a big one'.

GAMBIARRA [noun]   /gam-bee-AH-khah/

Sometimes when faced with a problem like having electrical wires dangling from the ceiling, you have two options. Either you go to the expense of calling someone out who will fix them up properly, redo the ceiling, charge you the Earth for it, but give you peace of mind that the problem is not going to come back. Or you take matters into your own hands and find a way to solve the problem yourself. Who needs electricians when a bit of masking tape can fix it all instead?

Any solution you find to a problem where you manage to do it yourself, making use of whatever tools you can lay your hands on, is called a *gambiarra*. Sure, it might look like a bit of a botched job and, realistically, all you've really done is kick the can down the road a bit, but for the time being you've fixed it.

Italian

Italian is one of those languages that always puts a smile on people's faces. Italian is the language of the opera, food, magnificent coastlines, art, and the beautiful towns and cities that line the length of the country. It's no wonder that Italy holds such a special place in so many people's hearts.

Italian is an extremely musical and melodic language. Rather than speaking it, it almost sounds as though people sing Italian as they raise and lower their pitch to emphasise different parts of the sentence, all accompanied by a visual feast of hand gestures, facial expressions and body language.

It's impossible to speak Italian without erupting into a big smile, because of the language's many open vowels and grammatical rhymes. Perhaps it's just that smiling is infectious, as Italians will be thrilled that you're interested in learning their language. They will most likely be very forgiving of any mistakes you might make and always try to help out where they can.

But Italian is by no means a small or insignificant language; 69 million people speak Italian as a first language, which makes it the third most commonly spoken language in the European Union, behind German and English.

Italy is an enormous country, known for its distinctive shape, with a population that is a similar size to the UK's. It is only connected to the rest of continental Europe at its very northernmost tip, where it shares a border with France, Switzerland, Austria and Slovenia. The rest of the country juts out into the middle of the Mediterranean as a huge peninsula, surrounded by the sea on both sides. It is over 620 miles (1,000km) long, but barely 250 miles (400km) wide. Its landscape varies dramatically, descending from the Alps it shares with Switzerland and Austria in the north, down through the vineyards of Tuscany, across the volcanic mountains of Naples and into the hot, southernmost tip of the Italian boot.

These geographic differences have led to population differences, too. Italy only became a unified country in 1861, after centuries of being divided into independent city states that didn't – and still don't always – see eye to eye. The legacy of this today can still be seen in language. Despite Italian being official everywhere, every town has its own accent, dialect and in many cases even its own local language. There is a standardised form of Italian which is largely based on the accent in Tuscany, but as many people will tell you, hardly anyone speaks that natively.

To many people, life in a sleepy Italian village eating delicious food out in the piazza every night and going to concerts at the local church sounds like heaven. But life in Italy has its complications, too. Since democracy was restored to Italy in 1946, the country has seen well over sixty different governments, meaning that it's rare to have a year when there are no general elections. The country has not fared well from the economic crisis, either, with many complaining about high inflation, unemployment and, of course, corruption.

But as we will see over the course of this chapter, these are simply the circumstances in which Italian life has learned to flourish. Italians are passionate about their culture and way of life and are always prepared for everything. So, if there ever were a country to look to as an example of how to steer through a crisis and come out smiling, Italy might be just the place to look.

MERIGGIARE [verb]   /meh-ree-JAH-reh/

Italy is a land of delights. Italians enjoy some of the greatest coffee in the world, some of the most enticing sweets and desserts known to man. Not only are they blessed with cities full of the most stunning architecture, but also landscapes filled with truly breathtaking scenery, all topped off with gorgeous weather. Italians know how to live well, but they also know that the secret to true lifelong happiness is also taking the occasional break. Especially if you make that break around midday and use it to doze off in the shade.

From there, the Italians gave the world the word *meriggiare*. It comes from the word *meriggio*, which means 'midday', and is the kind of thing you do on those perfect summer days just as the sun starts to get slightly too warm. Find a nice, cool, shady spot, close your eyes and drift off into a blissful little nap.

APERICENA [noun]   /a-per-ee-CHE-nah/

Mealtimes are an integral part of Italian culture. All the important things in life happen when you're sitting around a table with plates of exquisitely prepared food, which are bursting with bright colours and natural flavours, which you wash down with a glass of good wine. That's when people catch up with their friends, see their family, do business, discuss politics and set the world to rights.

But before all that, in Italy there's a ritual that might be even more important. When the guests arrive, you pour everyone a glass of something nice and pass around a few plates of salami, parmesan cheese, dips and other nibbles. That, is the *apericena*, which means the 'pre-dinner'. Sometimes your *apericena* can be so substantial that you don't even need to eat dinner, or *cena*, afterwards. This puts the aperitif, which is normally just a drink, to shame. It also has very little in common with that age-old English tradition of secretly scoffing a sneaky bag of crisps in the kitchen while the food's still in the oven. The *apericena* is when you start enjoying the pleasure of eating good food, drinking good wine and enjoying the good company of your friends and family before the main meal is ready.

CIOFECA [noun]   /cho-FEH-ka/

Italians appreciate true quality. It is the land of world-leading fashion, of top-class gastronomy, of fast cars, of tailors, designer sunglasses and perfumes. Yet despite this, the streets of most Italian towns will be lined with people selling almost identical-looking objects for knock-off prices on large white sheets that they can quickly grab and run away with at the faintest sign of the police arriving.

Those cheap handbags and sunglasses are not real. If you fall into the trap of buying one, you're going to end up with a *ciofeca*. A *ciofeca* is a fake, a poor imitation, or anything of really poor quality. You can also use it to refer to cheap wines, poor-quality foods and anything that doesn't actually live up to the high standards it professes to.

MENEFREGHISTA [noun]   /meh-neh-freh-GEESE-tah/

If you do end up buying yourself a *ciofeca*, though, not everyone will judge you. Like everywhere in the world, some people might look down on you for wearing odd-coloured socks, non-designer socks that cost less than €50 apiece, or even no socks at all. There are those who would rather die than imagine the thought of buying a supermarket pasta sauce in a jar instead of making their own. But in Italy there are probably at least as many people who see all of that is just unnecessary pretence and would rather stay clear of it all.

In Italian, if you're not the kind of person to get worked up about things and really just couldn't care less, then you are a *menefreghista*. This word comes from the Italian phrase *non me ne frega*, which means 'I don't care' or literally 'it doesn't rub me any'. *Menefreghisti* are the kind of people who no matter how much you try, they just won't get worked up about anything.

Given there are some things in life that are worth caring about, *menefreghista* is often also used in a negative way – to describe people who basically don't give a toss. But that, perhaps, is really just a question of perspective.

FARE LA SCARPETTA [phrase]   /FAR-reh la scar-PET-tah/

If you're a *menefreghista* who's quite happy to buy some shop-bought *ciofeca* pasta sauce probably without even bothering to think about what to serve for the *apericena*, then you're probably very unlikely to ever need this phrase. *Fare la scarpetta* is something that is reserved for true food lovers, who can't bear the thought that a gorgeous meal of sumptuous foods might at some point come to an end. People who *fanno la scarpetta* are the kind of people who savour every bite, close their eyes, express their delight by gesticulating wildly with whichever hand is not still holding their fork and emitting a faint groan, then desperately beg the chef to share their recipe with them so they can try to recreate that experience at home.

After all that, when the meal is done and just a few residues of sauce are left on their once-brimming plates, people who *fanno la scarpetta* will reach out and grab a huge hunk of bread, break it into pieces and dunk every one into whatever delights are left on their plate, swirl it around and keep the meal going for as long as possible. *Fare la scarpetta* is one of the most important of all Italian rituals: when you use bread to scoop up and finish off whatever's left on your plate.

ABBIOCCO [noun] /ah-BYOH-choh/

It's hard to say no to more food in a place like Italy, where everything's just so delicious. Italy is the kind of place where people take great pride in their flavours and there's no shame in dunking bread into sauces to make the tastes last longer. After a satisfying meal in Italy, nobody rushes down from the table to carry on with their busy lives; everyone is happy to linger for a bit. They enjoy the evening, the company of the people they're with, and if they've really eaten a lot they'll slip into a peaceful, drowsy daze as their bodies begin the tiring work of digesting everything they've just consumed. That satisfying drowsiness that sets in after a good, hearty meal has a name in Italy. It is an *abbiocco*.

MAGARI [conjunction] /ma-GA-ree/

Sometimes reality is just too predictable and monotonous. Sometimes we don't always want to think about the truth, but would be happier letting our minds wander and dream not just about the things that are, but the things that we want to be. This next word is about our imagination, our dreams and our aspirations. The Italian language can unlock that world of the 'if only' with just one simple word: *magari*.

Next time someone asks you if the Ferrari parked across the street is yours, just answer '*Magari*'. If someone asks you whether you own a seafront villa in Thailand with direct access to the beach, just answer '*Magari*'. *Magari* doesn't mean 'yes', and it doesn't mean 'no'. It simply means 'if only', or 'I wish'.

///

QUALUNQUISMO [noun]   /qua-loon-QUIZ-moh/

Many who visit Italy are seduced by the country's enviable way of life. Its exquisite vistas and enticing foods give the impression that Italy really is a piece of heaven on Earth. There is a long tradition of writers and artists from across Europe whose travels took them to Italy and who left their hearts behind there. But if there's one thing that might make life in Italy suddenly not seem so peachy it's this: politics.

Italy is constantly having fresh elections, new governments and bizarre laws, with corruption scandals erupting all over the place. These are the sorts of things that make many Italians want to throw their TVs out the window and never watch the news again.

But life must go on, and this next Italian word could prove to be a valuable gift to the English language, at a time when political instability seems to be taking root on the shores of the UK: *qualunquismo*. This roughly translates as 'the politics of whatever'. It's when you reach that point that you just couldn't care less any more. They all sound the same, they all look the same and they all break the same promises, so we might as well have any of them.

CELODURISMO [noun]   /che-lo-doo-RIZ-moh/

There is a certain unthinking, unforgiving male arrogance that few languages manage to adequately capture. It is the kind of thing that drives men to square up to each other and try to fight to defend their own pride. It's the same thing that stops them from asking for directions, or help when they can't find something at the supermarket. It's the state of mind that sets in when testosterone flies and men feel a sudden urge to prove – in case anybody had any doubt – that they are men.

In Italian, this kind of machoism is called *celodurismo*. It comes from phrase *ce l'ho duro*, which means 'to have a hard on'.

GATTARA [noun]   /gat-TAH-raḥ/

In Italy, old people are a respected and valued part of society. They wander around wearing nice clothes with shiny walking sticks and dazzling grey hair, stopping for the occasional coffee or glass of hard liquor so they can gossip with their friends in the square, and generally live quite happy and long lives. But, as in every country, in Italy there are some old people – particularly women – who decide that for their whole lives they've never really enjoyed the company of other people, and now that they're approaching the end of their lives they'd like to finally spend time with those feline creatures that truly do appreciate them.

Hence the word *gattara*, which refers to old ladies who live not just with cats, but for cats. Their whole existence is defined by cats. And they couldn't be happier for it.

PANTOFOLAIO [noun]   /pan-toh-foll-AI-oh/

There are many different types of people in life, all of whom enjoy doing very different things. There are the early birds rising at the crack of dawn and put on their running shoes, there are those who get up at a normal time and put on their work shoes, and there are those who perhaps prefer to get up a bit later, put on their slippers and don't really take their slippers off again until they go back to bed that night.

If that description rings a bell for you, then chances are that you're a *pantofolaio*, which literally means someone who stays in their slippers all day.

DONDOLONE [noun]   /don-doh-LOH-neh/

Perhaps you're neither an early bird nor a *pantofolaio*. Perhaps you get up in the morning and yes, you do put on your slippers, make yourself a cup of coffee, and go and sit outside on your balcony or porch and watch the world go by from the comfort of your rocking chair. As you rock back and forth, reflecting on the true meaning of life, perhaps deflecting some small-minded criticism you might receive from family and friends that you're sitting around 'doing nothing' all day, you might also reflect on the fact that if you are Italian, there's a name for you too. A *dondolone* means a 'rocker', but less in the sense of rock 'n' roll and more in the sense of rocking back and forth, and back and forth, and back and forth, in a very comfortable rocking chair.

CAVOLI RISCALDATI [noun]   /CAH-voh-lee riss-call-DAH-tee/

Italy has always been a favourite destination for honeymooners. How much more romantic can you get than the gondola, huddled with your loved one in a narrow wooden vessel propelled by a man dressed in stripes with a gigantic stick along the polluted canals of Venice? But perhaps that trip to Italy backfires. Maybe in that time you realise that you're not really meant for each other, and when you catch each other's eye at the baggage reclaim belt on your way home you realise that, in fact, something's not quite right.

If that happens and you do decide to end things, don't make the mistake of having *cavoli riscaldati*. Don't turn around six months later and say you regret everything and would like to give things a second chance. When you try to rekindle a relationship that clearly wasn't meant to last, in Italian that is called *cavoli riscaldati*, or 'reheated cabbage'.

PASSEGGIATA [noun]   /pass-edge-AH-tah/

Have you ever had that urge as the sun begins to set to grab your coat and go for a beautiful evening stroll? In Italy, this is what people who live in picturesque renaissance towns do. They stroll around the ornate streets, taking in the views, watching the colours, catching a glimpse of the nearby hills, and just as dusk begins to settle they gradually make their way back to sit down and have a nice evening meal. This is called a *passeggiata*.

CHE FIGATA [expression]   /keh fee-GAH-tah/

If you did set out on a *passeggiata* around your picturesque Tuscan village, you would no doubt be bombarded with sights so stunning that you would be left speechless by them. When Italians are so overwhelmed by just how awesome something is, they have a special expression: *che figata!* This literally means 'what a fig', paying homage to the queen of juicy and decadant fruits.

MOZZAFIATO [adjective]   /mot-sah-fee-AH-to/

However, if you truly are strolling about in an exquisite Italian town, the likelihood is that you won't even get a chance to utter an emotive '*Che figata!*' at the stunning sights that greet you. You will be so overwhelmed, so overcome by the beauty of the world that you won't just be speechless. It will be far more dramatic than that, as though somebody took the air as it was entering your lungs and sliced off your breath. When you've reached that state, you'll know that you are well and truly *mozzafiato*, literally 'to have had your breath cut away from you'.

Greek

Greek is one of the languages from which English has borrowed the most. The Greek language, with its ancient heritage stretching back many thousands of years, has always been there for English. Greek has given English some of its many complex and beautiful words to fill conceptual gaps that were otherwise missing from the Anglosphere, such as 'symmetry', 'icon', 'automatic', 'zone', 'graph' and, of course, 'democracy'.

Because of this legacy, for centuries people have been studying Ancient Greek. They became enchanted by the verse of Homer, the philosophy of Socrates and the prose of Euripides. Greece, it seemed, was a paradise of intellect, a world untarnished by the temptations and complexities of the modern world. And hence, there inevitably comes the moment when such classicists decide to make their pilgrimage to Greece, to walk the roads and admire the views as the Ancients once did.

When they arrive in Greece, however, they are greeted by a huge surprise as they discover that modern-day Greece is not quite the marble-polished, toga-clad, olive-branch-bearing utopia they had imagined.

Today, Greece is a wonderfully chaotic, vibrant and magical sort of place. Anyone who attempts the walks of Socrates around the ancient Athenian agora will instead find themselves in the midst of the winding alleys Monastiraki flea market, once an Ottoman bazaar, surrounded by endless hordes of Corinthian column replicas, ominously dark blue evil eyes and crowds of friendly street vendors offering to 'write your name in Greek' for just a few euros. They will navigate the treacherous terrain, where pavement merges unexpectedly into street café, and then back into two lanes of endless traffic. Perhaps they might eventually reach the main Monastiraki square, where they will find Athens's blindingly shiny, brand new metro and admire a truly stunning view of the ancient Acropolis, featuring a disused Ottoman-era mosque in the foreground.

Modern-day Greece is extremely proud of its ancient heritage. In Athens and Thessaloniki, you can hardly move nowadays for reminders of the past. When construction began on Athens's state-of-the-art metro system, so many ancient artefacts were found beneath the ground that in some places the architects decided just to leave the walls of the stations as glass, so passengers could peek in at some of the treasures that had been lying peacefully in the ground beneath their feet.

But there is another, extremely crucial side to Greek history, which is precisely what makes it such a fascinating place today. For in the thousands of years since its classical heights, Greece has been on something of a journey. Five hundred years of Ottoman Turkish rule have not gone unnoticed, especially as in that time populations became much more mixed and, for a while, people of different religions lived side by side. Thessaloniki, Greece's second city, is perhaps the best example of this, as although it is overwhelmingly Greek speaking now, just 100 years ago as much as 50 per cent of its population was made up by Ladino-speaking Sephardic Jews. It was also the birthplace of none other than Mustafa Kemal Atatürk, the father of the modern Turkish republic.

All of these things combine to make Greece the unique and beautiful place it is today. Greece is a crossroads, where European culture meets Eastern traditions and they merge to create a place that is recognisably East and West. In recent years, Greece has become Europe's frontier with the East, and for many millions of refugees fleeing atrocities at home it has been their first port of call after risking their lives in man-made dinghies to cross the narrow stretch of sea separating Greece's eastern Aegean islands from the Turkish mainland.

There is no better embodiment of Greece's history and crucial place in the world today than its language. To speak Modern Greek is to embark on a journey through time. You will construct sentences with words as ancient as human history itself, alongside exquisite Turkish loanwords that galloped across the plains of Central Asia towards the Aegean 800 years ago, dotted with words that didn't even exist a year ago.

The Greek language is the culmination of all these thousands of years of history, which have formed something truly beautiful and bursting with concepts, ideas and wisdom that English would truly benefit from. So let's take a look at some of those now.

ΦΙΛΟΤΙΜΟ / FILÓTIMO [noun]   /phil-O-ti-mo/

Since 2010, Greece has been afflicted by one of the worst financial crises in human history, crippling its infrastructure, impoverishing its pensioners and driving its youth to seek employment abroad. Yet despite the dystopian and uncertain world in which many people find themselves today, there has been a different side to Greece's financial crisis too. There has been a huge effort to help those in need, with people volunteering to set up foodbanks to give out hot meals and clothing to those who can't afford them.

These sorts actions towards strangers that come from a place of genuine kindness and generosity have a special name in Greek. They are *φιλότιμο* (*filótimo*), which literally means a 'love of honour'. *Φιλότιμο* is about treating others with respect and always doing the right thing. It's about putting others before yourself, and always fulfilling your obligations and duties towards others and society. If somebody has *φιλότιμο*, that means they will happily sacrifice their own honour and reputation for somebody else's sake.

ΜΕΡΑΚΙ / MERAKI [noun]   /mer-A-kee/

To do something with *μεράκι* is not just to do it well. Something done with *μεράκι* really is the result of a lifetime of passion, dedication and love. This word is a mark of respect to those who really pour their soul into what they do and who work really hard to achieve things even if they are difficult.

Yet often that desire to strive towards perfection can be exactly what destroys us, too. As a result, *μεράκι* has developed a secondary meaning describing exactly that feeling of sadness and hopelessness when something that you want is unattainable.

Μεράκι is originally an Arabic word (*maraq*) which has arrived in Greek through the Turkish word *merak*, meaning curiosity, passion and interest for something, but also depression and melancholy.

ΜΕΡΑΚΛΗΣ / MERAKLEES [noun]   /mer-ak-LEESS/

Closely related to *μεράκι*, a *μερακλής* is somebody who enjoys the finer things in life. He is a connoisseur who is well-versed in the many different luxuries and joys that life offers. He is the kind of person whose hand always shoots up whenever the waiter asks if anyone would like to taste the wine. This is somebody who really knows their stuff and appreciates things that are genuinely of good quality, or made with *μεράκι*.

A *μερακλής* can also be someone who not only enjoys that level of luxury, but also aspires to it in their own work, striving to do everything with good taste and attention to detail – a perfectionist, but in the most positive way possible.

ΛΕΒΕΝΤΗΣ / LEVENTEES [noun]   /le-VE-deess/

A *λεβέντης* is the kind of person all of us wish we had around the house when it's time to put shelves up. He is typically a young man who possesses outstanding qualities such as bravery and honesty. He's the kind of person who when the car won't start in the morning, or the trains are cancelled, doesn't collapse into a fit of despair and gloom. Instead, he sees a worthy challenge – a chance to test his skills and rescue people. *Λεβέντης* are always very tall, athletic and extremely well built.

The word *λεβέντης* is most likely another Turkish word. The Ottomans used the Turkish word *levend* to refer to the crews of their navy, when they were made up of non-Turkish sailors such as Greeks, Albanians, Dalmatians and other seafaring people under Ottoman rule. Some people, however, have suggested that the word comes from the Italian *levante*, meaning 'east', and was the way the Italians used to call the fleets of ships that sailed over from the eastern Mediterranean.

ΠΑΛΙΚΑΡΙ / PALIKARI [noun]   /pa-lee-KA-ree/

The meaning of the word *παλικάρι* is very similar to that of *λεβέντης*, except with one crucial difference: *παλικάρι* is the

Ancient Greek derived version and comes from the Ancient Greek word παλλάξ (*pallάx*), which meant 'young man'.

There's slightly more emphasis with the word παλικάρι on the fact that these men are particularly nice to look at. They are extremely handsome chaps, bursting with life, vigour and virility, and are an example to the world. They are also extremely brave and not do not shy away from challenges and hardship.

ΚΟΠΕΛΑ / KOPELA [noun]   /kop-EL-a/

When someone is too old to be a girl, but too young to be a woman, what would you call them? This eternal dilemma in the English language has caused many a scandal, and we still don't seem to be any closer to a word that we can all agree on. Calling someone a 'girl' after a certain age is patronising and 'woman' isn't always appropriate either. Meanwhile, 'young woman' or 'young lady' evoke fairly conservative connotations of finishing schools, which leaves us with a bit of a problem.

Here comes Greek with the perfect solution. Greek has a word that means neither girl nor woman, but someone right in the middle: *κοπέλα*. A *κοπέλα* is someone who is in the prime of their youth but no longer a child. Where this word comes from in Greek is not entirely clear, but some scholars have suggested that this one has been borrowed from Greece's age-old neighbours north of the border in Albania, where some dialects use the word *kopil* to mean a young woman as well.

ΚΕΛΕΠΟΥΡΙ / KELEPOURI [noun]   /ke-le-POO-ree/

Anyone who's been to Greece will be familiar with the difficulty of getting anything from your average Greek tourist shop. Those establishments that line the streets of any harbour or town centre are absolutely rammed with thousands of Spartan helmets, Socrates t-shirts, cat calendars, underwhelming watercolour paintings of ancient ruins and thousands of all sorts of other things that you never once in your life ever had any inclination to buy.

Yet every now and then, you might come across something that catches your eye and that you can even get a good price for. That one jewel, salvaged from the jungle of kitsch, is a *κελεπούρι*.

Once again, *κελεπούρι* was originally a Turkish word (*kelepir*), and has also developed a secondary meaning that refers more to people. Just like in those tourist junk shops, every now and then you come across someone who really sparkles. They might just be extremely good at their job and find themselves rising quickly through the ranks, or perhaps they're just the kind of person who's so rarely perfect in every single way that you want to cling on to them forever and marry them. Those people who really stand out are also called *κελεπούρι*.

ΚΟΛΛΗΤΟΣ / KOLLITOS [noun]   /ko-lee-TOSS/

There are some people in life that you're just inseparable from. At school, you'd forever be by each other's side, always spending time with one another. When you're not, you're on the phone to each other, talking through life's problems and advising each other on how to tackle big decisions. They are the type of friends you know you can always turn to, because they're never going to be very far away.

Your *κολλητός* really is your best friend for life, the one friend who you know you really couldn't live without. You are such good friends and spend so much time together that everyone says it's like the two of you are glued together. That is exactly what *κολλητός* means – someone who is 'stuck' to you. It comes from the word *κολλώ, (kolló)*, which means 'to glue'.

ΦΟΥΡΤΟΥΝΑ / FOURTOUNA [noun]   */foor-TOO-na/*

Sometimes life's problems really overwhelm you, and you start to feel totally lost at sea. A letter from the bank arrives out of the blue and knocks you overboard. You try to keep afloat but the waves keep coming, trying to knock you down. That, both metaphorically and literally, is what the Greek word *φουρτούνα* is about.

The *φουρτούνα* is a type of weather when there's a heavy storm and the seas get too rough. Boats get stuck in harbours, unable to sail, which can leave millions of inhabitants of Greece's many hundreds of islands totally stranded and cut off until it's safe for boats to go out again.

The word has also come to mean those times in your life when it feels like everything that could possibly have gone wrong has done and you're really struggling to cope. But it's not all bad though. There's a Greek expression that captures the essence of the challenge here perfectly: *ο καλός ο καπετάνιος στη φουρτούνα φαίνεται* (*o kalós o kapetánios sti fourtoúna fénete*), which means 'the good captain only appears in the *fourtoúna*'. In other words, whatever doesn't kill you makes you stronger.

ΠΑΘΑΙΝΩ / PATHAINO [verb]   /path-EH-no/

In English we have a fairly monochrome view of the way in which events take place. Things just 'happen', and it doesn't matter whether they happen *to* you, *because* of you or *in spite of* you, they all just 'happen'. In Greek, however, the fact that things can happen unjustly or cause unpleasant consequences, or even just be downright unpleasant, is not in the slightest overlooked.

The Greek verb *παθαίνω* is the perfect way to say that you're doing something, going to something or taking part in something, but that you're suffering immensely as a result. Most importantly, none of that is your fault.

If a parent sees their child crying, no matter what language they speak, they are going to be extremely worried and rush over. What they then say, however, seems to vary a lot depending on their language. In English they might ask the fairly neutral 'What happened?', or even the slightly accusatory 'What did you do?'. In Greek, however, the famously overprotective Greek mother will run to her child and cry '*Τι έπαθες;*' ('*Ti épathes?*'), which literally means 'What have you suffered?', which makes it incredibly clear that no matter what it was, it certainly was not the child's fault.

ΧΑΡΜΟΛΥΠΗ / CHARMOLYPI [noun]   /khar-mo-LEE-pee/

The Greeks, who claim to have invented drama and tragedy, know very well that sometimes emotions are complicated. Some things make you want to laugh and cry. Sometimes you can be really happy for somebody else, but deep down very sad inside, like that day when your eldest child leaves for university, or your other half gets that job they wanted but it's in another city and you're left wondering whether or not you should go with them or stay put.

In Greece, trying to get in touch with your innermost thoughts is a national pastime. People do not shy away from these sorts of emotions and face them head on. They create a language in which they can speak to people about them, which makes everything a lot easier to deal with. This word is the perfect example of that. *Χαρμολύπη* is a combination of the words *χαρά* (*khará*), meaning 'joy', and *λύπη* (*lípi*), which means 'sadness'. It literally means the co-existence of both joy and sadness when something happens, and is a beautiful way to acknowledge that sometimes in life it's all right to feel conflicted.

ΚΑΗΜΟΣ / KAIMOS [noun]   /ka-ee-MOSS/

The Greeks know that of all the range of emotions available to humankind, the most powerful and most dangerous ones are those that burn. As a result, they have the word *καημός*, which comes from the word *καίω* (*kéo*), 'to burn', which can mean several different things. Its first meaning is, again, one of depression, heartbreak and a particular kind of pain that deliberately targets the soul. However, *καημός* can also be used to describe unfulfilled and unrealistic desires. Its final meaning is a deep and very pressing desire to do something, such as 'I have *kaïmó* to go and travel around the world'.

ΓΡΟΥΣΟΥΖΗΣ / GROUSOÚZIS [noun]   /groo-SOO-zeess/

Some people in life are lucky, and no matter what happens to them they always seem to land on their feet. If they drop a glass, it will just bounce off the floor in one piece.

Then there are those who only need to look at a wine glass for it to break. They don't even need to check which side their toast fell on, because they know it'll be the buttered side. They don't bother washing their cars, because they know seconds later they'll be visited by a flock of migrating pigeons with stomach problems. These people are not just unlucky, but they attract bad luck. They are cursed to break things, to go on holiday and have a week of bad weather, and generally to go through life without feeling like the sun is ever really shining on them. That person is a *γρουσούζης* (*grousoúzis*), which is a word that comes to Greece via its neighbours in Turkey.

ΞΕΡΟΣΦΥΡΙ / XEROSFYRI [noun]   /xe-ro-SPHEE-ree/

In Greece you always drink alcohol with food. Even if you just order a beer, you'll always get a little bowl of peanuts, crisps, pistachios or something to nibble on. In English, we call that cheating.

However, there are some in Greece who – perhaps influenced by drinking habits in the UK – choose not to have anything to eat with their drink. Instead, they'll drink on an empty stomach, or in Greek: *ξεροσφύρι*. This literally means 'dry whistle', and is what you need to tell your waiter if you don't want any meze with your glass of ouzo. It's also what you'll need to say if you have to explain to people why you're feeling so rough the next day.

ΞΕΝΥΧΤΩ / XENYCHTO [verb]   /xe-nikh-TO/

Nightlife in Greece is much more important than daylife. Greek therefore boasts an extensive and colourful set of vocabulary that can describe everything that happens after the sun sets, the temperatures dip, the night cicadas start their peaceful tune, and all across Greece streets, harbours, beaches and bars become packed with people heading out to let their hair down. That time of the evening …

Although in the UK pubs traditionally close at 11 p.m., in Greece you'll struggle to find anywhere that's even open yet at that time. People will just be finishing their meals and gradually thinking about heading over to a bar, which will be totally deserted before at least 2 a.m. anyway. Hence the need for the word *ξενυχτώ*, which comes in very handy in Greece, and means 'to stay up all night partying'. But don't worry, if you know how to play your cards right, this doesn't need to be as hectic as it sounds. The trick is to take a very long and peaceful nap just after lunch in the heat of the day, around that time when all you'll see wandering the streets is mad dogs and Englishmen anyway.

fighting and ethnic cleansing that Europe had seen since the Second World War. Nowadays, Yugoslavia is no more, and neither – technically – is the Serbo-Croat language.

Nowadays, Croatians speak Croatian, Serbs speak Serbian and Bosnians speak Bosnian. But a Bosnian can speak Bosnian to a Croatian, who can reply in Croatian, and a Serb might overhear and mutter something in Serbian, and everyone still understands everyone. Just like an Irishman from Dublin can talk to a Canadian from Vancouver while being overheard by a South African from Port Elizabeth and nobody has any problems understanding anyone.

So why does nobody talk about Serbo-Croat any more?

The story of Serbo-Croat or, as it is now known, Bosnian/ Croatian/Serbian, is a classic story of where politics and language cross. For each of the countries of the former Yugoslavia, the most important thing was to have a separate and distinctive national identity. For centuries in Europe, national borders have tended to be drawn along linguistic lines. And so even though the language spoken in Zagreb is as different from the language spoken in Belgrade or Sarajevo as the English in Boston is to the English in Glasgow, as Yugoslavia fragmented into different countries, three new languages were born: Bosnian, Croatian and Serbian. However, as all three languages remain highly mutually intelligible and – according to some linguists – even variations of the same language, it makes sense to still group them together for this chapter. However, nowadays the convention is to refer to each of them in alphabetical order as Bosnian/Croatian/Serbian, or BCS for short.

The distinctive features of BCS are that they all belong to the southern group of the Slavic language family, and due to many years of Ottoman occupation they all received a lot of influence and loan-words from Turkish. Since the break-up of Yugoslavia, however, Croatia in particular has been prolific in trying to 'purify' its language, finding Slavic equivalents for foreign loanwords and thus quite demonstrably differentiating itself from the other two. Croatians, therefore, borrow books from the *knjižnica* or 'book place' while Serbs and Bosnians go to the *biblioteka*, and they play *nogomet* while Serbs and Bosnians play *fudbal*.

Yet Serbia's landlocked positioning has led to influences that never quite reached the other parts of Yugoslavia. Modern-day Serbian has taken on a surprising number of loan-words from its northern neighbour Hungary, such as *šargarepa* (Hungarian: *sárgarépa*) for carrot, while Croatians and Bosnians eat *mrkva*. To make things even more interesting, Serbian is the only language in the world that can be officially written in two alphabets, either Latin or Cyrillic. Croatian and Bosnian, on the other hand, are always written in Latin, although due to the large population of Serbs in Bosnia, many signs there are still written in both.

Whatever you want to call it, the Balkans is a fascinating and often overlooked part of Europe. No matter what language they speak, everyone in the region is united by their love of music, dancing, good food and lethal alcoholic spirits. Despite its troubled past and at times uncertain future, the Balkans is a place where you live life to the max and, as we'll now see, its languages have gathered a plethora of valuable wisdom as a result.

SIKTERUŠA [noun]   /sik-teh-ROO-shah/

Hospitality is taken very seriously in the Balkans. Inviting or being invited round to someone's house is seen as a great honour, and your hosts will be eager to show their kindness to you by making you food, anddrinks, and making sure you really feel welcome and part of the family.

Often you will be offered coffee, which might be boiled over a stove with plenty of sugar in a tiny metal vessel, as it is in many places where the Ottoman empire set foot. But sometimes people will make their guests coffee, even though they have absolutely no intention of letting them stay for a long time, and will perhaps even make this abundantly clear to them. They might take a while to actually get round to making it, they might be stingy about the biscuits and fruits they serve with it. Or they might *not* make themselves a coffee and just stare at you while you drink yours until you leave. This confusing hospitality which is not quite hospitable has got a special word in Bosnia: *sikteruša*.

RAHATLUK [noun]   /rah-hat-LOOK/

Those days are the best: when the sun is shining, you're outside enjoying an iced coffee or some kind of meaty pastry, you're done with your work for the day and you're looking forward to catching up with friends and family later on that evening. You feel as though you haven't a care in the world.

When you reach that point, it's truly precious. Make sure not only that you hold on to and cherish those feelings, but that you know what to call it. In BCS it is called *rahatluk*. Unsurprisingly, this word for when everything feels sweet, creamy and moreish is actually very close to the word *rahat lokum*, which is another name for Turkish delight.

FJAKA [noun]   /FYAH-kah/

Mindfulness is such an integral part of life now that it's impossible to call it a new craze. But since a series of books, apps, podcasts and videos hit the web making people aware of how important it is to make space not just for their bodies but also for their minds, life has changed significantly. Companies now take mental health seriously and awareness around the issue has rocketed everywhere.

Croatians might argue, however, that they were on to the topic long before it went viral. They would point to the fact that their language has long had the word *fjaka*. This word refers to the state of total relaxation of body and also of mind. It's when you're lying on a sunbed, staring out over the turquoise waters of the Dalmatian Coast below, and absolutely nothing worries you. You're relishing in the luxury of doing absolutely nothing, with no stresses or cares in the world. That is *fjaka*, which is a bit like the Italian *dolce di far' niente*.

MERAK [noun] /MEH-rak/

In Serbian, *merak* is not about driving fast cars, wearing fancy clothes, eating in the most expensive restaurants, or living the life of luxury. It's not about counting how many digits there are in your bank balance or showing off to your friends about that new yacht you bought. *Merak* is not even about saving up to buy the latest smart phone or trying to derive happiness in any way from things that cost money.

Merak is about something far simpler and far humbler. It's about feeling the warmth of the spring sunshine on your hands as you walk towards the railway station in the morning and smiling. It's about looking up and catching the most exquisite colours and patterns from the sunset, projected on to the clouds above you. It's about the taste of a nice cup of coffee at 11 a.m. *Merak* is when you feel happy, contented and can derive pleasure from all of the simplest and everyday things in life.

MILOZVUČAN [adjective] /mee-loh-ZVOOH-chan/

Over the course of a friendship, there are moments when you discover things about your friends that you might never otherwise have guessed. One of these revelatory moments may be when you and your friends first step into a karaoke bar together. Before long, it will be known to all just how badly you can actually sing.

But you might be surprised. One of your friends might open their mouth and pure beauty will come out. They may in fact be gifted with the most beautiful voice in the world and actually turn out to be a real hidden talent. You may even ask them to sing again and again and again.

Some people are just gifted with beautiful voices, and not just when they sing. In Croatian, those people who have the kinds of voices you want to fall asleep listening to have a special word: *milozvučan*, which translates roughly to 'sweet-voiced'.

INAT [noun]   /EE-nat/

Imagine a world without pride. Not pride in the positive sense of taking pride in your community and that sort of thing, but of unnecessary and egotistical pride, the kind that leads people to do unfathomably stupid things. Imagine a world where people don't decide to 'take things outside' in a pub because someone knocked into the other person's wife. Imagine if people didn't feel the need to prove a point, no matter how damaging it was to themselves, simply to protect their egos.

Unfortunately, that way of thinking is as integral a part of the world we live in as the sun rising and setting every day. People have egos, and people will go to all sorts of lengths to prove their points. In English we might talk about 'cutting off your nose to spite your face', which demonstrates the issue at hand quite graphically. But in Serbian there is a word that directly describes the adamant, unrelenting and obstinate pride that lies behind that act. What is it that drives people to cause others harm, even if it means that they're going to get harmed themselves? In Serbian, it's *inat*.

MUDA LABUDOVA [noun]   /MOO-dah LAH-boo-doh-vah/

We live in an imperfect world, and sometimes those imperfections can get so frustrating that we lose touch with reality. We find ourselves asking for things that we can't get, like exiting an international treaty but asking to keep all the bits we like. It's a bit like going to the supermarket, buying a trolley full of groceries, and then asking the check-out assistants to pack it all into one bag, but not to make that one bag too heavy to carry. It's like baking a delicious Victoria sponge cake and putting it out on your kitchen table for all of your guests to see in its perfection. Although you want people to see and admire it, you also want to eat it. But if you eat it, nobody will be able to come and see it.

The truth is, some things in life are simply beyond the realms of possibility. No matter how much we ask for them, bargain over them, or stomp our feet about them, we simply can't ask for the impossible. Because in Croatian, those things are *muda labudova*, which in other words means 'swan's testicles'.

KOŠTANIK [noun]   /KOSH-tah-nik/

In the Balkans, eating is a hugely important part of the culture. Mothers, grandmas and aunts like to stack the plates high and watch people enjoying their cooking. Traditionally, it's always been seen as a good thing to be quite round and well built, even though this might contradict some modern conventions around beauty.

For students, who grew up in the countryside but then moved to the cities to study and work, this leaves them with a particular dilemma. In the city they'll try to keep their weight down and keep fit. But when they're back home, they'll be scolded by their families for being so thin and be given punitive extra portions of whatever's being served to set things right. When they return to the city, they'll be faced with the task of trying to take all the weight off again, just in time for their next trip home to the village where they'll be fed and start the cycle once again.

When someone is incredibly skinny, so much so that you can almost see their bones, you would call them a *koštanik*. This comes from the word *kost*, meaning bone, and literally means 'someone made of bones'.

ĐUSLA [noun]   /JOO-slah/

Historically, such was the importance of not being too skinny in Balkan culture that this way of thinking is even codified into the language. This next word is one that some Serbs might not recognise from the language today, because it is slightly older than the others, but that makes it no less applicable to the world today.

This next word is the opposite of a *koštanik*. This is no size-zero model, this is instead a lady with serious curves. She is strong, she is well built and not exactly the kind of person you would want to mess with. But at the same time, she is beautiful, desirable and feminine. She loves who she is and she's not afraid to flaunt it. She is, of course, a *đusla*.

LILA [noun]   /LEE-lah/

Buying a new mobile phone is an enormous source of anxiety and unnecessary stress for many people. You either hand over a significant chunk of your bank balance up front to possess this thing that you know in just a few months will look old, cracked and outdated, or you sign a legally binding contract that will force you to own it for the next two years of your life, come what may. But once you've come through that first hurdle of deciding which phone you want, and whether or not you suspect you're being ripped off, next comes the real anxiety: not dropping it.

Once you've got that first crack in the screen, you can breathe out a sigh of relief knowing you're on a downward slope to normality, but until then it's quite stressful. Nowadays, to add to that stress, smartphones come with that special thin layer of plastic over the screen that's very easy to peel off, and some people leave it there until it falls off naturally to try to prolong their phone's chances of survival.

But what would you call that layer? Perhaps the thought of it causes so much trauma that we choose not to name it in English, but Serbian has an excellent word that might apply. Whenever there's a thin layer of anything that's quite easy to peel off, that's not just another layer. That's a *lila*.

ŠTREBATI [verb]   /SHTREH-bah-tee/

It's no secret that we in the UK feel slightly shy about our foreign-language abilities, and as a result many of us do not consider that we speak any as adults. Despite this, though, many of us have at least pretended to learn French, German, Spanish or something during our school years. We sat with pieces of paper and memorised the days of the week for vocabulary tests. We wrote out elaborate paragraphs about our daily routines, memorised them, and recited them by heart in oral exams, as though we were having some kind of genuine conversation. And then, as we left the exam room, all of that knowledge simply fell out of our heads, never to be retrieved again.

Perhaps there's something about the exam system that encourages short-term knowledge acquisition, rather than long-term learning, but whatever it is, we all know that it's a problem. The first step to solving that problem is to recognise it, and this is where Croatian can help. The verb *štrebati* in Croatian means 'to memorise something off by heart for a test and then immediately forget it'.

GLABATI [verb]   /GLAH-bah-tee/

Vegetarianism is viewed by some in the Balkans with deep mistrust and suspicion. Although life for those who choose to abstain from animal flesh is somewhat easier in bigger cities nowadays, in the countryside the idea of not eating meat is simply anathema to centuries and centuries of life there, despite the consequences. In Croatia alone, meat consumption in 2009 was at nearly 150lb (70kg) per person, making it one of the most carnivorous countries in the world. In Serbia, heart disease is by far the largest cause of death and premature death, much of which is linked to the country's high rates of red meat consumption.

Nevertheless, countries don't change their habits overnight and people in the Balkans will always love their meat. So much so, in fact, that they even have a special word for when the meat you've just eaten was so delicious that you pick up the bones and gnaw at them, even if they have no meat left on them. That is called *glabati*.

DANGUBITI [verb]   /dan-GOO-bit-ee/

One of the greatest joys of being a student is the holidays. You can wake up at midday without any shame, roll out of bed, spend all day watching junk TV, maybe stumble out in the evening to see your friends somewhere, then go back to bed and repeat. They are the days in which you can do absolutely nothing, which is a kind of true bliss.

Working adults can have similarly pointless days, but the difference is that they must at least have the veneer of seeming productive. They can spend their whole day working on proposals that are so fundamentally flawed they won't get off the ground; they can spend all day putting up shelves that once they put the first object on them will crash to the ground, undoing the whole day's work; they can spend all day filling out forms only to find that because they missed one box the whole thing is invalidated and they have to start again.

What do you call it when you spend your whole day doing something totally pointless? In the Balkans there is a particularly concise word that captures precisely that: *dangubiti.*

UHLJEB [noun]   /OOKH-lyeb/

It is sad that so much in life is not about what you know, but who you know. Yet all over the world, this tendency exists. Unfortunately, the Balkans is not a part of the world that is exempt from this system, and as a result connections are extremely important. So much so that just like in so many other of the languages we've seen, there is an entirely special set of words and vocabulary to quite capture just how frustrating life in the world of nepotism can be.

The Balkan equivalent of the old English saying of 'If you can't do anything else, teach, and if you can't teach, teach PE' might be more along the lines of 'If you can't do anything else, ask your uncle if he can have a word with the minister and get you a job in the civil service.' Those people who are entirely underqualified for their jobs yet hold public service positions because of who they know, is *uhjleb.*

POLJUBITI VRATA [phrase]   /poh-LYOO-bit-ee VRAH-tah/

All social occasions these days have to be meticulously planned with plenty of warning. Even just meeting someone for a coffee will require a plethora of emails, texts, phonecalls and any other type of communication available before you're able to settle on a time and a place that suits both. What happened to the good old days when you'd just go round, knock on someone's door and see if they're in and fancy a chat?

Of course, what we forget about those good old days before we had mobile phones that could reach anyone anywhere on the planet was how much time we'd waste. We'd spend hours sitting in cafés, wondering whether people were even going to show up. We'd drive up and down the same street a million times trying to work out whether the house numbers were going up or down because we didn't know where we were going. And, of course, we'd spend quite a bit of time standing outside people's houses knocking on the door, wondering whether they're even in.

When you do go round to someone's house, knock on the door and then, after a while spent convincing yourself that actually no, they're not in, return home, that little expedition has got a special name in the Balkans: *poljubiti vrata*. This literally means 'to love the door', because you spend so much time face to face with it.

HUNGARIAN

Right in the heart of Europe lies one of the continent's greatest linguistic mysteries. Hungarian is like no other language. Despite the fact that it is surrounded by Slavic languages to the north and south, German to the west, and Romanian to the east, Hungarian is so different to these that it sometimes seems that it must have landed there from outer space.

This gives Hungarians an enormous advantage in the world. Wherever they go, they can feel safe in the knowledge that nobody will be able to understand their outrageously dry sense of humour and pointed remarks about everyone around them. Unless they have the misfortune of bumping into another Hungarian, of course.

The origins of the Hungarian language are hotly contested and remain largely unknown to this day. What we do know is that the first Hungarians arrived in modern-day Hungary just over a thousand years ago, most likely from somewhere in Central Asia, where they had close contact with a people called the Turks, who made their way to what is modern-day Turkey at around the same time. Hungarian, therefore, has some links to Turkish, as it does to Finnish and Estonian. But nowadays these commonalities are so ancient and tenuous that – unlike Czechs and Slavs, or Spaniards and Italians, who with a bit of effort can at least read each other's languages – no Hungarian can ever really make themselves understood in their own language anywhere outside Hungary.

Hungary's positioning right at the crossroads of Europe, where north meets south and east meets west, meant that Hungarians have always been in close contact with their neighbours. Throughout history they have been occupied by various different empires. Efforts were often made to marginalise Hungarian in these times in favour of the occupiers' languages, which meant that for a long time Hungarian was not used in Hungarian courts, schools or any official contexts. But in the nineteenth century a group of Hungarian writers and intellectuals decided to replace the German that was used across official life in Hungary by creating an enormous quantity of brand new Hungarian words and terms, many of which are still in use today. This important moment in Hungarian history is known as the *nyelvújítás*, or 'language renewal'.

One of Hungarian's most notable characteristics is that it is an agglutinative language. That means that you can simply keep adding more and more things on to the ends of words until you finally end up with what you want the word to mean. Hungarian word order is also completely flexible and customisable to suit you. That means you can change around the order in which words come in a sentence however you like, in order to emphasise or de-emphasise an idea, or make a particular pun or word play.

Hungarian is an incredibly creative language, in which people come up with new words all the time, and it gives full freedom to its speakers to express themselves however they want. It's therefore also an extremely colourful language, with a rich and incredibly unknown literature, as much of it has not been properly translated to this day. All of this contributes to the fact that, despite really being smack in the middle of Europe, to most Europeans much about Hungary and Hungarian remains an enigma.

HÁZISÁRKÁNY [noun]   /HAA-zee-shaar-kaan(y)/

After a long, hard day out at work, the one thing that might quicken your step slightly as you make your way home in the evening is the thought of seeing your other half. You'll greet them with a kiss on the cheek and sit down to a nice meal with them and tell them all about your day. That is, of course, unless you have the misfortune of living with a *házisárkány*. In that case, you'll stay at work as late as possible, accidentally miss your stop on the bus and walk for as long as possible before you go home and face your *házisárkány*'s fiery wrath.

The Hungarian word *házisárkány* literally means a 'house dragon', and if you happen to live with one you'll understand why. Your *házisárkány* is your extremely impatient and ill-natured spouse. They're always nagging at you for not doing the washing up, not using coasters, forgetting to do the DIY, not taking the rubbish out, or anything else on the interminable list of sins that will make your dragon roar. Be wary of the *házisárkány*, they breathe fire.

DONALDKACZÁZÁS [noun]   /DON-ald-koh-chaa-zaash/

Everyone has different ideas about their ideal Sunday: some like to get up at the crack of dawn and go out and exercise in nature, some like to clean the house, some like to go and read books in a nice coffee shop, and some of us just like to open a can of beer and recline on the sofa in front of the TV all day wearing nothing but a t-shirt.

Hungary is a landlocked and mountainous country, with roasting hot summers and heatwaves that can go on for weeks and months. In those summer months, *donaldkaczázás* is not just a fashion statement, it's a way to survive. *Donaldkaczázás*, which means 'being like Donald Duck', is when you just wear a t-shirt and nothing else, just like Donald Duck. Perhaps those of us who enjoy the odd *Donaldkaczázás* need a good *házisárkány* to keep us in check.

PIHENTAGYÚ [adjective]   /PEE-hen-ta-djoo/

I once stayed with a family where the mother had a very set routine. Because there were a lot of people in the house, there would always be a long queue for the bathroom in the mornings, so every day without fail as she left the house she would take a bag full of her make-up in one hand and the rubbish in the other. She'd throw the rubbish away, then get in her car, drive off to work, and do her make-up whenever she got a chance at a red traffic light. One morning, though, as she left the house with the two bags in each hand, she tossed her make-up bag into the rubbish bin and only realised when she reached her first traffic light that she had the rubbish bag on her lap, stinking out the car. She then couldn't throw that bag away until she finally got to work and could stop.

That moment in Hungarian is what you would describe as *pihentagyú*. It means 'resting brain' and refers to those times when your brain just gives up on you and you do totally stupid things out of the ordinary.

KAPUNYÍTÁSI PÁNIK [noun]   /KUP-oon-yee-taa-shee PAA-nik/

When people reach a certain age, panic can set in. They realise that life is not going to last forever, and as they gradually confront their own mortality, they make rash decisions. If they don't buy that sports car now, then when else will they get the chance to roar down the street, screeching to a stop at every road bump, making all the neighbours turn and stare at them?

In Hungarian, that feeling – the mid-life crisis – is called a *kapuzárvási pánik*, or literally 'a fear that the gate is closing' like the German *Torschlusspanik*.

However, your mid 40s is not the only time when you can feel overwhelmed by life. Another common point is your mid-20s, when, after a lifetime of having everything clearly defined and decided for you by parents, teachers, peers and the institutions that you've always belonged to, you find yourself out in the real world. You're paralysed by the thought of all the different things you could do, and the crushing reality that you have to make choices and won't have time to do everything as you watch your youth trickle away.

In Hungarian, that time when young people are suddenly faced with the reality of life for the first time is called *kapunyítási pánik*. This literally means 'a fear that the gate is opening'. You can try to shut it again, but those hard decisions will still be waiting for you on the other side.

TÜKÖRSIMA [adjective]   /TUU-ker-shi-ma/

Despite having no direct access to the sea, Hungary has the next best thing, which is Lake Balaton, Europe's largest freshwater lake, stretching for 48 miles (77km) and with an average depth of 10ft (3.2 metres). It is about an hour and a half to the west of Budapest; Hungarians flock to Balaton in the summer with buckets, spades, swimming costumes and sun cream, and sit and drink beer and wine spritzers, eat fried dough with cheese, sour cream and garlic called *lángos*, kick back and enjoy what they fondly call *a magyar tenger* – 'the Hungarian sea'.

Because Balaton is a lake, though, and not a sea, there are many moments when it is completely still and hardly a wave laps against its shores. On a clear, sunny day the surface of Balaton is a stunningly perfect baby blue light, and if you stand on the southern shores and look across to the lavender fields of the Tihány peninsula, you can see a perfect reflection of the land on the water's surface.

In Hungarian, that view, when the water is completely still and perfectly reflects the shore like a mirror, is called *tükörsima*.

ARANYHÍD [noun]   /UH-rung-heed/

When Lake Balaton isn't enough and Hungarians need the alternative beauty and unpredictability that the sea brings they usually travel to neighbouring Slovenia and Croatia to see it. At some point on these trips, the Hungarian language captured another concept that has slipped many other cultures by. That moment when the sun begins to set over the sea and the sky starts to turn a deep orange colour, it forms a perfect, glistening white path reflecting on the surface of the water from the shore all the way out as far as the eye can see. To Hungarians, that is an *aranyhíd*, which means a 'golden bridge'.

PUSZIPAJTÁS [noun]   /PUSS-ee-pie-taash/

As in all big cities, people in Budapest have a reputation in Hungary for not always being the friendliest of people, especially to tourists, visitors and anyone they don't know. If you smile or acknowledge the presence of someone in Budapest on the street in any way, as you might in a village or small town in the countryside, you will be greeted with alarm and almost certainly declared unstable and dangerous. But when people in Budapest spot somebody that they do know, they couldn't behave more differently. They stop, say hi, hug, kiss each other, ask how the other person is doing, and make plans to go for a drink and catch up with them properly soon.

Centuries of foreign invasion and occupation have left Hungarians fairly suspicious of those they don't know, and so it can take a while before a Hungarian will warm up to you. But once they do, and they reach the point that they do feel like they can stop and say hi to you and kiss you in the street, you will become their *puszipajtás*. This literally means a 'kiss pal'. It indicates precisely that level of friendship when it's OK to stop and kiss each other in the street. However, there's still a way to go after this point before you reach true friendship, mind.

PERTU [noun]   /PER-too/

Budapest is famous for its *romkocsmák* (ruin pubs), which are drinking establishments that sprang up in the many old, abandoned buildings that once littered downtown Budapest. Generally outside in the sun, with swings and beanbags and brightly coloured benches to sit on, these places offer a creative and bohemian alternative to the stuffier pubs that we're used to drinking in in the UK, and many foreign visitors tend to lose their minds when they see how much cheaper things are than back home. As a result, many owners have grown wary of large groups of tourists, unfortunately particularly from the UK, and have even put signs up outside to put them off.

Nonetheless, drinking is an important part of Hungarian culture. Hungary boasts an impressive range of locally brewed frothy beers and lethal homemade fruit-based spirits known as *pálinka*. But until recently it was a huge taboo in Hungary to clink glasses. This dates back to the revolution of 1848, when the Hungarians tried but failed to overthrow their Austrian rulers. The story has it that after the Austrians crushed the dissent, they celebrated in Vienna with a toast and clinked glasses. The Hungarians vowed that they wouldn't clink glasses again for 150 years – and, until 1998, they didn't.

Now that the taboo has passed, though, this Hungarian word can come back into fashion. A *pertu* is that precious moment when you signify your friendship with another person by sitting down in a *romkocsma*, looking each other in the eyes, knocking your two glasses together and declaring '*egészségedre*', which is Hungarian for 'cheers'.

POLGÁRPUKKASZTÁS [noun]   /POL-gaar-pukk-us-taash/

Some people want an easy life with a two-up, two-down somewhere not too far from the city with fluffy carpets your feet will sink into on a Saturday morning and a wall-mounted TV. Other people find the very notion of that nauseatingly boring and dedicate their entire lives to doing things to shock and horrify those machine-washable members of the bourgeoisie to the point that they explode.

In Hungarian, anything you do that shocks bourgeois people so much that they explode is called *polgárpukkasztás*, which literally means 'citizen popping'. For something to be *polgárpukkasztás*, it really has to make ordinary people freak out. Shaving your hair into a pink Mohican and putting piercings everywhere you can imagine and then walking into a supermarket and doing your daily shopping among middle-class people fainting at the sight of you is pretty *polgárpukkasztás*. Spraying a wall with obscene graffiti can also be quite *polgárpukkasztás*. Anything can be *polgárpukkasztás*, to be honest, as long as it breaks the rules of society and causes horror.

ÜGYESKEDŐ [adjective]   /UUD-jesh-kedd-oooh/

Geopolitics following the Second World War left Hungary on the other side of the Iron Curtain, as part of the Warsaw Pact along with Poland, the Soviet Union and Czechoslovakia. In many ways, communism hit the country hard and people were often short of resources that people took for granted in Western Europe. Hungary made several unsuccessful attempts to release itself from Moscow's grip, most infamously in 1956 when the people of Budapest rose up against their Soviet occupiers only to be crushed by tanks and brutal military force. The scars of those days are still visible on many of Budapest's beautiful, crumbling old buildings today, and it was not until the fall of the Berlin Wall that Hungary re-joined the Western world.

At a time when resources were scarce, people in Hungary had to make do with what they had, which was an occasion to use one of Hungarian's most apt words: *ügyeskedő*, which means when you do the best job you can with the least possible effort.

RENDÜLETLENÜL [adverb]   /REND-uul-et-len-uul/

It's great to have interests in life, but it's better to have passions. If you like reading, don't just pick up a book every now and then, flick through it and then put it down never to open another one for months or years. If you like cooking, don't just buy all your food from the frozen section of the supermarket and heat it up in the microwave. If you like travelling, don't go anywhere near a package holiday office and book whatever overpriced trip they try to flog you. Instead, read books and don't stop reading. Find new books by unheard of authors and read them again and again. Read books as you walk down the street. Likewise, go down to your local farmers' market and find the most bizarre produce you can and cook it for people. Become a master of the kitchen. Become the person everyone wants to be invited round to dinner by. And explore the world, going to places you can't pronounce and nobody has ever heard of. Go off the beaten track and have unique experiences that no tour operator has ever dreamt of.

Those things show true passion and indicate that you don't just have a passing interest in whatever you're into but that you've embraced it with your heart and soul and made it a part of who you are. That attitude, that feeling and that state of mind has a special word in Hungarian: *rendületlenül*.

ELKELKÁPOSZTÁSÍTOTTALANITOTTÁTOK [verb]

/EL-kel-kaa-poss-taash-eet-ot-tal-an-it-ot-taa-tok/

Hungarian savoy cabbage farmers (*kelkáposzta*) may often be faced with the horrendous problem of when their savoy cabbage crops get overgrown. Wading through the fields, with savoy cabbage everywhere, unable to see the ground, what on Earth are they to do?

Fortunately, Hungarian has a word: *elkelkáposztá-sítottalanitottátok*. This word roughly translates to 'you people have now cleared away the weeds of the savoy cabbage'. One of Hungarian's greatest assets is the fact that it is possible to construct almost any word by putting any combination of words together to make something that to Hungarian speakers will still make sense. This comes in particularly handy when trying to create words for specific problems that require specific solutions.

MEGSZENTSÉGTELENÌTHETETLENSÉGESKEDÉSEITEKÉRT

[unclassified]   /MEG-sent-sheyg-tel-en-eet-het-et-len-sheyg-esh-ked-eysh-eh-it-ek-eyrt/

If you thought *elkelkáposztásítottalanitottátok* was the longest or most useful word in Hungarian, though, then you'll find it's already been dwarfed by another even more complex word. In Hungarian, you just keep adding bits on to the end of words in order to express more information, like prepositions, tenses, people and so on. So the wonderful Hungarian word *megszentségteleníthetetlenségeskedéseitekért* came into being, which translates as 'on account of the fact that you people continue to behave as though it is impossible for you to be desecrated'. Quite what the context for using this would be remains something of a mystery.

BELEKOSTÓLNI [verb]   /BEH-leh-kosh-tole-nee/

Hungary boasts a colourful and unique cuisine of delicious stodgy stews and dishes that are all packed full of spice, flavour and paprika. *Gulyás*, or paprika stew, is famous the world over and is one of the things Hungary is best known for. There are also all sorts of other things that are perfect for warming you up on a freezing cold Central European winter's day, all with sauces and stews that you cannot resist dipping your finger into to have a quick taste of before they're served up.

Doing that, which no doubt in most social circles is a serious faux pas, is popular enough in Hungary to even have its own word: *belekostólni*, which means to dip your finger into a stew or sauce and have a quick taste before you start eating.

KÉRNI [verb]   /KAYR-nee/

Asking for something is a rather clunky and awkward experience in English which causes learners and native speakers alike plenty of angst and stress. You can't just 'ask' for something, because that would seem presumptuous and rude. In many cases, even just asking for something and then plonking the word 'please' on the end doesn't quite cut it either. So your safest option is to resort to rather awkwardly navigating around with long and clunky expressions like 'Could I possibly trouble you for ...' and 'Is there any chance you might have ...' and so on.

Hungarian looks at these English problems and laughs. In Hungarian, there's a much more pragmatic understanding of the fact that there are occasions in life when you need to ask for things. As a result, they have the perfect verb to deploy at these times: *kérni*. It means 'to ask for something politely'. So instead of saying 'Could I please possibly ask you for a cup of coffee, if that's not too much to ask', in Hungarian you can just say '*Kávét kérek*', which in effect means exactly the same thing.

POFA [noun]   /POH-fah/

We Brits, like the Hungarians, can be a little bit reluctant to really show how we feel. Unlike the culture of southern Europe or even Germany, where people see no problem in being fairly to the point about expressing how they feel, we tend to avoid showing our true feelings, preferring to tell people what we think they want to hear. However, sometimes our faces do the talking for us and show exactly what it is that we're unwilling to actually say.

Being able to decode those facial expressions is a vital skill that will enable you to succeed in life. The Hungarian language recognises this and offers the world the word *pofa*, which means 'the meaning behind any given facial expression'. In other words, the *pofa* is not what you're saying, it's what your face is saying for you.

Dutch

The language of the Netherlands is called Dutch. This is a historic error that the English committed and to this day have still never corrected. Dutch is probably what we should be calling German, because the Germans call their language '*Deutsch*'. The Dutch also call German '*duits*' and their own language '*nederlands*'. But despite this, English persists in getting the two confused.

Many people in the UK also mistakenly refer to the Netherlands as 'Holland'. Holland is a small yet significant part of the Netherlands, like Yorkshire or Surrey. The Dutch call their country '*Nederland*', which if translated means 'low country'.

The Netherlands is a small and flat country across the North Sea from Britain. It is famous for its national obsession with bicycles, tulips and mild-tasting cheese. The Netherlands has always been seen as an extremely progressive country, due to its liberal and tolerant stance on issues such as cannabis, legal prostitution and other things that until very recently would have made your average Englishman blush.

Yet despite its small size, the Dutch were at one point keen merchants and sailors, who travelled and colonised the world. They took spices and natural resources from places as far as Indonesia, the Caribbean and South Africa, and brought them back to Europe. The Dutch were even some of the first people to set foot in what is today the United States, establishing the settlement of New Amsterdam, which after being captured by the British was renamed New York. Nonetheless, parts of the USA retain a visible cultural link to the Netherlands, with New Yorkers being referred to as Yankees because it sounded like *Jan Kaas*, Jan being a common Dutch name and *kaas* meaning 'cheese', and many old American families having Dutch surnames.

The Dutch spread their language too. To this day it is spoken in the Caribbean and Surinam, a small country on the northern coast of South America. At one point, Dutch was also widely spoken in South Africa. However, due to contact with other African and Asian languages, the language has now evolved into something distinct called Afrikaans. The Dutch claim that they can still understand this fairly well. South Africans think otherwise.

Dutch happens to be one of the easiest languages for English speakers to learn, as it's one of the closest living languages to English. Only Frisian is closer, which is a language spoken in the very north of the Netherlands. All you need to do is get your head around Dutch's colourful yet consistent spelling system and you'll easily start recognising words like *goed* (good) and *huis* (house).

In this chapter we'll take a look at some Dutch words that you may not recognise, although the concepts that lie behind them should hopefully be familiar enough!

GEZIN [noun]   /khe-ZIN/

In English, the word 'family' can be a very broad and ambiguous concept. Does it refer just to your immediate family who you live in the same house with? Or can it also include your cousins, nephews, uncles, in-laws, or simply anybody you share DNA with?

Dutch makes a very neat distinction here and has two words, both of which can be translated into English as 'family'. Your *familie* is anyone who is related to you. This is the huge umbrella term that encompasses the entire family tree. Those people that are closest to you, though, like your parents, your siblings and your children, are quite neatly distinguishable by calling them *gezin*. That makes it a lot clearer what you mean when you talk about keeping things 'in the family'.

OCHTENDHUMEUR [noun]   /OKH-tuhnd-huu-meurr/

Some of us are morning people. We leap out of bed in the morning, rain or shine, make nutritious smoothies and skip to work radiating an infectious sense of self-fulfilment and joy. For others, even just the thought of the sun rising, our alarm going off and having to start another day with our jumper on backwards and the trains all cancelled fills us with existential dread. That second kind are the people you'd better avoid at the coffee machine for fear of injury.

In English, if you're not a beaming ray of sunshine every morning, you might rather unfairly get called 'grumpy', when in fact you're only like this specifically at early times in the day. Dutch is much more understanding of this. If you're the kind of person who needs to be given some space in the morning until you've reached the coffee machine, and even better until you've come back from your lunch break, then don't worry. You just have *ochtendhumeur*, or a 'morning mood'.

VERONGELIJKT [adjective]   /fer-ON-khe-layeekt/

If you are somebody who has *ochtendhumeur*, you will be familiar with the great injustice of being called grumpy or unfriendly, when all you really need is caffeine. Being misunderstood in this way is hugely frustrating, and almost belittles the fact that so many of us are just not morning people. When people try to say otherwise, you are within your rights to feel a specific type of indignant anger that someone has done something wrong.

But what on Earth do you call that feeling? It's more than just being 'wronged', because what that person did wasn't just 'wrong', it was totally outrageous and unacceptable. Only the Dutch word *verongelijkt* can really summarise exactly how you feel. This is when you have suffered an injustice; someone has said or done something totally wrong, and you need to set matters straight.

TAALGENOOT [noun] */TAHL-khe-note/*

The Netherlands is a relatively small country, and Dutch is a relatively small language. It is spoken in the Netherlands and by the majority of people in Belgium, where it is called Flemish. As a result, in order to get by in the world many Dutch people have learned exceptionally good English that even puts many English speakers to shame. Dutch people often seem effortlessly bilingual, and have a reputation as some of Europe's greatest linguists.

Yet there is always something special about being able to have a conversation with someone in your mother tongue. When you speak a language like Dutch, this can end up actually being a very rare treat. So when you do come across someone who also speaks the same language as you, you have a special bond. In Dutch, that person would be your *taalgenoot*. This literally means your 'language comrade' and is the person you turn to when you get tired of speaking foreign languages and just want to give your mouth and your brain a bit of a rest.

GEZELLIG [adjective] */khe-ZELL-ikh/*

The streets of Amsterdam can be a harsh and unforgiving place in the depths of winter. When the canals are frozen over, the freezing fog is setting in and it looks like it's going to snow, you need somewhere you can go to warm up. Across the city are little cafés and pubs that can just about fit a bar, some comfy chairs and a nice warm fire where you can feel at home. These places are so cosy, so comfy, so warm, and make you feel so happy, that they cannot really be described by any English word. In Dutch, they are called *gezellig*.

But *gezellig* can also be that warm fuzzy feeling you get about something when you know you're having a nice time. You can get it from feeling at home somewhere, and you can also get it from having a good chat with an old friend over a glass of beer in the summer by the canal. It's a feeling that's overwhelmingly happy, positive and makes you smile inside.

SNEUVELEN [verb]   /SNOW-vull-uh/

In the old days of the Dutch empire, many young people went off to fight overseas in the army. Unfortunately, many never returned, having died on the battlefield. Yet to simply say that they 'died' does not really do them justice in the eyes of the patriot, for whom to sacrifice one's life for one's country is the highest form of honour. As a result, when describing such tragic events the Dutch word *sterven*, meaning 'to die', seems almost inappropriate. They gave up their lives for a cause, an idea and a way of life that unfortunately they would never live long enough to see fulfilled. In Dutch, people who fall in battle and die in honour have their own word: *sneuvelen*.

The good thing about the word *sneuvelen*, though, is that nowadays you can use it quite freely for all sorts of trivial things. If you drop your book in the bath and all the pages crinkle and the ink runs, you can say your book is *gesneuveld*. If your car breaks down on a motorway on top of an enormous dyke after many years of loyal service, then your car has also *gesneuveled*. *Sneuvelen* is a respectful way to say that something is gone, but went honourably and will never be forgotten.

DROOGZWEMMEN [verb]   /DROH-kh-zveh-muh/

The next word is a tribute to a slightly cautious worldview. When you're learning to swim, you have two options. In English, we might 'throw you in at the deep end' and leave you to work everything out for yourself. In Dutch, you take a more sensible approach. Before you even touch the water, you spend some time at the side of the pool learning all of the moves and practising them from the safety of *terra firma*. This is called *droogzwemmen*, or 'dry swimming'.

Nowadays, the Dutch like to *droogzwemmen* everything. When you want to check that a system is working before you release it, you *droogzwemmen* it too.

SWAFFELEN [verb]   /SWUFF-uh-luh/

When Dutch teenagers finish school or university, they – like their British counterparts – like to go off into the world and travel around undiscovered places that they then realise other people hadve already discovered. They hang out with people their age from all over the world and take advantage of their newfound freedom to do the kinds of daredevil activities that their mothers would rather *sneuvelen* than find out about. The gap year (or 'gap yah') is a chance for young people to work out what they want to do with their lives and to find out a bit more about themselves.

British travellers don't have the best reputation for behaving well overseas, but sometimes the Dutch really give them a run for their money. In 2008, Dutch newspapers were full of reports that a Dutch student had been arrested in India, because he'd *swaffeled* the Taj Mahal. This caused an absolute outrage in the Netherlands – and of course in India, where the *swaffelen* had taken place.

In the rest of the world, however, people were slightly bemused. What is *swaffelen*? And how can a word that sounds so funny cause so much offence? Once people found out what *swaffelen* meant, though, it was no laughing matter. *Swaffelen* is the curious habit of rubbing your genitalia against something.

VINDPLAATS [noun]　　　/FIND-plaah-ts/

If you are a somewhat forgetful or distracted person, you will be familiar with what it's like to be dressed and ready to leave the house, but about to spend half an hour playing hide and seek with your house keys, your car keys, your bus ticket, your phone, your shoes, your gym pass, or whatever else it is you always seem to manage to lose.

The great thing about trying to find things, though, is that they always manage to be in the last place you look. In Dutch, there is a specific word for the place in which you find anything. It is *de vindplaats*, or 'the finding place'. So next time you're hunting around the house, looking for something you've lost, just remember that you need to work out where its *vindplaats* is.

KNAAGSELS [noun] /KNAAH-kh-sells/

Sometimes when you want a snack, in English you might be offered 'nibbles'. 'Nibbles' are usually small, crunchy and insignificant little things that you can have to satisfy your appetite for a while and just nibble on gently while you have a drink or wait for a meal. But what if you want something much more substantial than that? What would you ask for if you don't want just want to nibble but actually want to, say, gnaw on something?

This sort of dilemma does not exist in Dutch, because they have the word *knaagsels*. This literally means 'things you can gnaw on' and refers to much harder, tougher snacks like rusks and biscuits and things that are going to keep you busy for quite a long time.

UITWAAIEN [verb] /OWT-vah-yuh/

There's nothing more frustrating than writer's block. Staring at a blank page or computer screen, willing the words to write themselves, completely at a loss as to how to break the barrier between the vague images you have in your head and the way in which you need to phrase them in order to pass them on to other people. You can spend hours in this place, trying to find a way past it.

Sometimes all you need to do is close your laptop, stand up and go for a walk. This will clear your head, put fresh oxygen into your body and bring you a fresh new perspective on whatever it was you were working on. Before you know it, you'll feel much less stressed, far calmer and able to put your mind back to whatever it is you need to do. In Dutch, when you take that brief walk or break from a stressful activity to clear your mind, that is called *uitwaaien*, meaning 'to blow out'.

UITBUIKEN [verb]   /OWT-bow-kuh/

There are a handful of occasions in the year when it is socially acceptable to eat so much you feel like you might explode. The most common of these is around Christmas time, when people gather in families to stuff their faces, load up on comfort food and celebrate having passed the darkest day of the year.

Exploding from overeating is a messy and undesirable affair, though, and so the Dutch language recommends that you take far more sensible measures in order to avoid it. If you feel as though you are at risk of bursting after a heavy meal, simply push yourself back from the table, exhale, loosen your belt by a few notches and just let everything hang out. In Dutch this is called *uitbuiken*, which literally means 'to belly out'.

MELIG [adjective]   /MAY-likh/

The Netherlands is known for being a progressive and liberal country, and one of the things that most symbolises this is its tolerant attitude towards cannabis. Although not technically legal in the Netherlands, no police time is spent on enforcing this rule, and cannabis is available for purchase from special coffee shops just about everywhere. However, you're more likely to find tourists in most of those coffee shops than locals, because despite the *de facto* legalisation of cannabis far fewer people in the Netherlands smoke it than do so in the UK.

This word is not necessarily to do with drugs, but does refer to that state of hysteria you can reach when you discover something that is just so funny that you can't stop laughing. When you get the giggles, and no matter what you look at you just burst into uncontrollable fits of laughter, so much so that you might have to leave wherever you are, Dutch has a special word for you: *melig*.

GERMAN

The longest word in the German dictionary is *Donaudamp-schifffahrtselektrizitätenhauptbetriebswerkbauunterbeam-tengesellschaft*, which by any measure is ridiculously long. At eighty letters, it also knocks any English contenders, such as 'antidisestablishmentarianism', well and truly out of the park.

But importantly, the *Donaudampfschifffahrtselektrizitäten-hauptbetriebswerkbauunterbeamtengesellschaft* is no joke. It is a word that a German speaker genuinely created, in order to express the highly nuanced concept of the 'Association for Subordinate Officials of the Head Office Management of the Danube Steamboat Electrical Services'. Such is the genius of the German language that such a thing can be expressed in one single word.

German may not be the first language to come to mind when thinking about the most beautiful language in the world, but the true delights of German are reserved for those who learn it. German is a remarkably expressive, witty and creative language. It is less guttural than Spanish and far easier to spell than French. It was once known as the language of poets and thinkers, and indeed it boasts an impressive array of native speakers whose writing has changed the world we live in.

Millions of British tourists visit Germany every year to see its serene dark green forests, brooding lakes and picture-postcard villages. Others go to photograph what's left of the Berlin Wall and to traipse through Berlin's hedonistic nightclubs.

In recent years, an unprecedented number of young Brits have gone one step further: they've taken one look at the quality of life enjoyed in Germany, plus the far lower cost of living, packed their bags and settled there permanently.

In the twenty-first century, the world has a lot that it can learn from Germany. Equally, the English language has a lot that it could learn from its not-too-distant cousin, German.

German is a disarmingly sardonic language that manages at the same time to be both incredibly sophisticated and outrageously farcical in its sense of humour. German is the kind of language in which you can ridicule people for parking in the shade, throwing snowballs with gloves on, or taking a warm shower. In German, you confront life's problems with an armful of sizzling bacon and find solutions to them over a staple bottle of schnapps.

AKTIVANSTEHER [noun]   /ak-TEEV-an-shtay-er/

The Brits may like to think of themselves as world leaders in the art of queuing. They derive a masochistic pleasure from standing patiently behind people who they know will, as a result, get better seats than them on the bus, or be served faster than them at the pub. Yet despite British queuing expertise, there is a glaringly obvious gap in the associated vocabulary. The true art of queuing is not just about patience and good manners, but also about efficiency. In other words, the real point of the queue is to get out of it as quickly as possible.

In German, the *Aktivansteher* is the energetic queuer. This has little to do with energy, however, and everything to do with those people's astonishingly fast way of getting through lines. The *Aktivansteher* can spot which queue is moving faster from a mile off. They can apply the right amount of pressure to ensure that the people in front keep moving along, without even dreaming of stepping out the line to pick up that ingredient they forgot from the back of the supermarket. The *Aktivansteher* is the Porsche of patience, the pinnacle of precision, the master queuing tactician.

FINGERSPITZENGEFÜHL [noun]   */FING-er-shpit-sen-ge-fuel/*

There is competence, and then there is *Fingerspitzengefühl*. Despite how it may sound, this word has nothing to do with spitting kerosene on your fingers. If somebody has *Fingerspitzengefühl*, it means they have an inherent talent and expertise for doing something. They literally have a 'feeling in the tips of their fingers' for what they are doing, which is why they are so good at it. Their excellence is not learned, it is instinctive and unparalleled.

But more than just expertise, when something is done with *Fingerspitzengefühl* it is also done with the maximum tact and discretion. *Fingerspitzengefühl* is the kind of quality you would ideally look for in somebody whose job it is to negotiate a bold and destiny-changing treaty on behalf of their country.

KUMMERSPECK [noun]   /KOOM-mer-shpek/

Sometimes in life things don't go to plan. Relationships can combust, organisations can go bust and deadlines can come hurtling towards you at a million miles an hour as you realise in horror that you have no Plan B. We may have our own ideas in the UK of how to deal with these problems, but in Germany people reach for the nearest packet of bacon, or *Speck*. The weight of uncertainty can dramatically alter our behaviour and push us into habits that we know are bad for us. If one of those habits is eating things that ordinarily you would not, you may find yourself putting on a few extra pounds.

In German, that unwanted weight that comes on during periods of high stress is known as your *Kummerspeck*. Literally, this means 'worry bacon' and refers to that excess weight that collects around your sides and hips.

WALDEINSAMKEIT [noun]   /VALD-eye-n-zam-kite/

Germany has infinitely more woodland than the UK (a whopping 32.7 per cent forest coverage versus 13 per cent in the UK). Due to the fact that the UK is a lot smaller than its German neighbour, much more deforestation has taken place there, meaning that if you want to experience this next German word without straying too far from home, you'll have to work a lot harder.

Germany is covered in lush forests, such as the *Schwarzwald* (Black Forest), with lakes and streams all bursting with untouched nature. All of this plays a large part in German life and in the German psyche, which gives rise to the concept of *Waldeinsamkeit*. This literally means 'forest isolation', or 'forest loneliness'. This is when you need to get away from the rhythm of your daily life, say goodbye to traffic jams and rush hour on the tube and go off to reconnect with the world, hiking through the woods for days without seeing another soul and feeling at one with Mother Nature. It is a refreshing, detoxifying experience. It is perhaps the original German answer to mindfulness.

FERNWEH [noun]   */FERN-vay/*

Brits have an unfortunate reputation when they're abroad, of being rather fond of their home comforts. That's why, in tourist areas that appeal to British tourists, the world over, you'll see signs advertising a cooked English breakfast and a pint of lager. That is called 'homesickness', which in German is *Heimweh*.

But what about when you open your curtains in the morning and groan at seeing the grey clouds outside? What about when the familiarity of walking into a restaurant and being able to understand everything on the menu stops being comforting, but starts being boring? And what about when you don't want to bump into people you know but want to start finding out more about people that you don't?

German has the perfect word that summarises all of these things: *Fernweh*. This is the desire to be far away, to travel, to break with your routine, to discover new places, meet new people and try new things. It is about being open to the wider world, desiring to learn more about it. Perhaps it's not a surprise that Germans are some of the world's most prevalent and adventurous travellers.

OHRWURM [noun]   */OR-vurm/*

The eventful summer of 2017 was memorable for many reasons. Yet what will stick in most people's minds is the soundtrack of Puerto Rican singer Luis Fonsi, featuring Daddy Yankee and Justin Bieber, and their record-breaking hit 'Despacito'. For months, the reggaeton song accompanied every moment of it in cafés, bars, restaurants, shops and just about anywhere you could imagine, all over the world. People would find themselves humming it while waiting at traffic lights, taking the lift, in the shower and everywhere. Even though the song was primarily in Spanish and most people couldn't understand what it was about, it burst into people's heads and occupied their subconscious the whole summer. Now what on Earth do you call a song that does that?

In German, a song that is just so catchy that you can't get it out of your head is called an *Ohrwurm*. This means an 'ear-worm' and refers to the way in which a song like that will crawl in, slowly and gradually, until you just can't get rid of it.

HÜFTGOLD [noun]   /HUEFFT-gold/

The German language understands that people can't enjoy an endless diet of sausages, cake and beer without it having some sort of impact on their waistline. Yet German does not lament this fact. Instead, those who love their food are celebrated. Rather than seeing that little bit of extra weight that people carry around on their hips as negative, in German it is referred to as *Hüftgold*, which means 'hip-gold'. You can also refer to it as *Hüftspeck*, or 'hip-bacon'.

SEITENSPRUNG [noun]   /z-EYE-tun-shprung/

In keeping with the candour and matter-of-factness that characterises the German language, the word *Seitensprung* literally means a 'leap to the side' and refers to when a happily married German decides to pursue a love interest outside of their marriage. In other words, this is an affair or little infidelity, yet the word *Seitensprung* feels much more like a small deviation than a scandal. There may be some correlation between this attitude, though, and the fact that polls by Durex, IFOP and some dating sites state that around 45 per cent of Germans admit to pursuing an extramarital affair, which is one of the highest incidences in Europe.

DRACHENFUTTER [noun]   /DRA-khun-foot-ter/

If you do make the mistake of springing a *Seitensprung* on your German spouse, don't expect to get off scot-free. In fact, the rage that Germans suffer at the hands of their spouses is so well documented that the Germans even had to invent a word with which to quell it: *Drachenfutter*, or 'dragon feed'. *Drachenfutter* are those nice flowers you buy on your way home from work, that surprise reservation you made in that fancy restaurant in town, or that time you decided to spontaneously clean the oven. *Drachenfutter* is a gift to assuage anger – anything that douses the flames of angry rage of the *Drachen*, or the dragon that you keep at home.

NOTGEIL [adjective]   /NAUGHT-guy-ll/

In the spring when the sun starts shining again, the flowers begin to bloom, the birds are singing, the bees are buzzing and the world breathes out a huge sigh of relief that the cold and darkness of the winter are gone, something else also starts to happen. People experience a deeply primitive and hard to suppress urge to reproduce. It can happen at any time and in any place, but what most characterises it is its urgency and also its unpredictability.

The German language captures this kind of feeling perfectly with the word *notgeil*. This comes from the word *geil*, which confusingly manages to double up and both refer to the carnal urges of humankind, and stand in as a less loaded positive adjective that can loosely be translated as 'cool'. The German prefix *not–* is even more confusing. *Not–* does not mean 'not', but emergency, and therefore *notgeil* apparently refers to that irrepressible urge to have sex. A word of advice though: don't try using this as *Drachenfutter* if you are planning a *Seitensprung*. It will not suffice.

WARMDUSCHER [noun]   */VAHM-doo-sher/*

Of all the things that can go wrong in your home, boiler problems are most definitely the most frustrating. Especially during the winter, when you can spend ages standing by the shower, tentatively sticking your hand under the water and telling yourself that you can manage a cold shower on that freezing February morning, then realising that you can't and waiting a bit longer in the hope that the water will warm up.

Unfortunately, waiting for your shower to warm up is not yet a widely accepted excuse in most cultures for being late for work, but in Germany it is especially frowned upon. If you are the kind of person who will only wash in warm water, there is even a specially reserved, pejorative term for you. You are a *Warmduscher*. This literally means 'warm showerer' and in other words means that you're a bit of a wimp. You may quite justifiably wonder why this can serve as an insult, when the vast majority of people in the world probably do prefer to shower warm, but that's the kind of thing that only a *Warmduscher* would say.

HANDSCHUHSCHNEEBALLWERFER [noun]   /HAND-shoe-
schnay-ball-ver-fer/

In a similar vein, a *Handschuhschneeballwerfer* is the kind of
despicable coward that would throw a snowball at someone
while wearing gloves. Again, you may argue that that is perfectly
reasonable, but not in German, you 'gloved-snowball-thrower'.

SCHATTENPARKER [noun]   /SHATT-uhn-pah-ker/

Breaking with the theme of embracing the cold, a *Schattenparker*
is the kind of unforgivable wimp who can't handle the infernal
heat of their car after leaving it all day in the sun and so parks in
the shade. Because, surely, the sign of true virility is the person
who will park in the middle of a blazing hot car park and then
simply not suffer as they melt in the furnace that awaits them
when they return and try to drive off again.

TURNBEUTELVERGESSER [noun]   /TOURN-boy-tel-fer-
gess-er/

For some of us, doing sport and PE at school was quite a
traumatic experience that we tried to avoid at all costs. The
most successful of us would master the art of forging a sick
note from a parent or guardian. The less successful would
try the age-old trick of pretending to have forgotten our
gym kit. In German, those who pull that trick are known as

Turnbeutelvergesser, or 'gym-bag-forgetters', and would normally have to suffer the humiliation of doing sport anyway, but with kit retrieved from the dreaded lost property box.

More broadly, a *Turnbeutelvergesser* is someone who shows signs of disorganisation, is a bit of a dreamer and seems unable to remember the practical things in life. They're the kind of people who are a bit slow and a bit dull, who flake out on plans, but always seem to have some sort of feeble excuse at the ready.

SITZPINKLER [noun]   /*ZITS-pink-ler*/

But by far the most unforgivable of all of these crimes must be the *Sitzpinkler*. The *Sitzpinkler* is someone so spineless, so weak and so unmanly that they sit down to urinate. You may hope that women would be exempt from this accusation for biological reasons, but don't count on it.

BACKPFEIFENGESICHT [noun]   /*BACK-pf-eye-fen-ge-zikht*/

If you ever come across somebody who parks in the shade, sits down to urinate, throws snowballs with gloves on and turns the heat up in the shower (if they've remembered their gym bag, that is), then that combination of crimes can only lead to them being one thing: a *Backpfeifengesicht*. This word literally translates as 'a face in need of a back-handed slap'. If you are ever called this in a German-speaking country, run.

SCHNAPSIDEE [noun]   /SHNAPS-i-day/

A *Schnapsidee* is an epiphany brought on by sitting in a pub one rainy Sunday afternoon with friends and enjoying a few pints. Literally, it is a 'schnapps idea'. No doubt there have been *Schnapsideen* that have changed the world, but in German generally the word refers to the other kind of inebriated, effusive enthusiasm for a plan that will never get off the ground but sounded Earth-shatteringly brilliant and viable at the time of conception.

TREPPENWITZ [noun]   /TREPP-un-vitz/

Sometimes the greatest comebacks and wittiest remarks come to us after the event, when the person we'd most like to say them to is well and truly gone. Had an uncomfortable meeting with your boss in which you struggled to defend yourself, only to have thought of the perfect rejoinder as you were on your way out? That's classic *Treppenwitz*, or 'staircase wit'.

KOPFKINO [noun]   /KOPF-kee-no/

But the beauty of *Treppenwitze* is that even if you might not have been able to use them in real life, you can always play the scene out in your *Kopfkino*, where you get to decide what happens next. *Kopfkino*, or 'head-cinema', is when you sit and try to think through what would have, should have and could have happened. *Kopfkino* is when you relive moments, or plan for eventualities to help you make a decision. *Kopfkino* is when you play things out in your head, but with 3D glasses and surround sound.

///

TORSCHLUSSPANIK [noun]   /TOR-shlooss-pah-neek/

Certain opportunities in life don't always hang around. Sometimes you can't just put off trips until next year, turn down job offers until you feel ready to move, or keep dating endlessly until you find the one. Sometimes you just have to go for it, before the doors are closed. That feeling of anxiety that perhaps you might be about to miss out on a great opportunity, those ten seconds you have left to squeeze through before the doors finally shut, is called the *Torschlusspanik*, or 'gate-closing-panic'.

///

STRAHLEN WIE EIN HONIGKUCHENPFERD [noun]
/SHTRAH-len vee eye-n HOH-nik-koo-khen-pferd/

In English you might grin like a Cheshire cat, but in German when you have that ear-to-ear smirk of delight you are said to *strahlen wie ein Honigkuchenpferd*, or 'beam like a honey-cake-horse'. The German beautifully captures the sickly sweetness of a honey-cakey grin with the aloof gormlessness of a horse, to make a word that would certainly not go amiss in the English language.

Swedish

There are about seventeen or eighteen different vowel sounds in Swedish, each of which can carry one of two different tones. This helps the whole language to sound to the untrained ear as though it carries the melody of a beautiful song.

Sweden's most successful music group, however, didn't sing in Swedish. Like most people in the enormous yet sparsely populated Scandinavian country, the singers of ABBA spoke flawless and practically unaccented English, having no problems switching between the two. Of all countries in the European Union, Swedish high school graduates are the most likely to leave school with a working proficiency in English.

This leaves Swedish in an interesting position. Whenever there are high levels of bilingualism in a country, people tend to use the languages for different purposes. They may speak to foreigners in English, do business in English and read websites in English, but Swedish, naturally, remains extremely close to their hearts. They therefore keep Swedish to one side, reserving it for a particular kind of humour and to express particular types of concepts and ideas that simply don't translate that well into other languages. It is precisely those types of words that this chapter is going to uncover.

Most people around the world have at least a passing familiarity with the Swedish language, thanks to the unparalleled success of a certain discount furniture store. Despite operating in almost fifty countries around the world, flat-pack furniture giant IKEA clings adamantly to its Swedish roots and makes sure not only that all of its stores are painted in the blue and yellow of the Swedish flag, or that every customer has a chance to sample Sweden's trademark meatballs and gravy with lingonberry jam, but that almost every single item of furniture has a long and unpronounceable Swedish name. This gives Swedes the chance to chuckle at people struggling to ask for the *oumbärlig* frying pan (which in Swedish means 'indispensable'), the *knubbig* ('chubby') table lamp or the humorously named *fniss* rubbish bin ('giggle').

Such are the privileges of speaking a small language. With just under 10 million speakers, it's an exclusive club, which means not everyone can be in on the joke. But despite its elusive appearance, Swedish is not as far from English as it might first appear. Both are Germanic languages and, thanks to a series of Viking invasions, many Swedish words will seem eerily familiar to English speakers. 'To come' in Swedish is *komma*, and the phrase 'where do you come from?' sounds like *var komma du ifrån*, which is not a million miles away.

Caution should be exercised, though, before assuming that Swedish and English are too similar, as there are plenty of traps. Swedish *kissa* may sound like 'to kiss' but actually means 'to pee', and the Swedish word *bra* means 'good' ('bra' is *behå*).

Outside of Sweden, you'll find some Swedish speakers in Finland, where Swedish is an official language and widely taught in schools. You'll also find that people in Norway and Denmark won't struggle too much to understand Swedish, and some people in Iceland might be able to have a go too.

Swedish is a beautiful language, and Sweden is a place that captures the imagination of nature lovers, interior design fanatics and human rights activists alike. So let's take a look, now, at some of the words that Sweden has to offer the world.

JOBBIG [adjective]   /YOBB-ig/

Among much of Europe Sweden has an almost utopian reputation for being a place that just works. Sweden has one of Europe's most enviable social systems and is famous for its progressive policies on issues such as shared parental leave and gender equality. This often begs the question: what is it about that sparsely populated, enormous country full of forests in the heart of Scandinavia that just seems to get so many things right?

Well, Swedes might not necessarily think that they got to where they are overnight. Because, of course, they didn't. To get to where Sweden is now requires plenty of work. That is a concept that is made explicit in Swedish by this word: *jobbig*.

If something is *jobbig*, then it's not easy. In fact, it's quite the opposite. It's hard and tiresome to deal with, and requires a great deal of patience and willpower in order to get done.

SKÄMSKUDDE [noun]   /SKEM-skud-duh/

Nobody likes cringe TV. When someone goes in for a kiss and the other person turns away, leading to an endless dialogue of people establishing the fact that they really weren't on the same page at all, it's the kind of thing that will invade your living room with a vengeance, daring you to keep watching, daring you to keep suffering with the awkwardness of what just happened, or rather didn't happen.

Those moments are when you want to grab the nearest cushion and cover your face with it until the awkwardness has passed. In Swedish, that fluffy protective shield against everything awkward is known as a *skämskudde*, or literally a 'shame cushion'. It can also be used metaphorically for when you see awkward things in real life and find yourself cringing inside and out and want to just stick your head in the sand and never come out.

MASKROSBARN [noun]   /MASS-kros-barn/

Our childhood is one of the most formative times in our lives. It's one for exploring the world, learning about right and wrong, discovering what it means to be loved and love others, and setting off on the amazing adventure that is life. Ironically, though, it's also the time of our lives over which we have the least influence and control. As children we really have little power to influence the direction in which our childhood will go, which means that for some of us childhood is not always the happiest of times. All sorts of things can make life really tough at that age, and it can take a long time, even as adults, to begin to sort all those things out.

Yet sorting things out is what many people who've had more challenging childhoods manage to do. They deal with things and move on. They flourish into wonderful human beings and go on to have amazing lives. Those children who have a tough time but in the end turn out all right are called *maskrobarn*. In Swedish, this literally means a 'dandelion child'.

FIKA [noun/verb]   /FEE-kah/

Sweden has some of the world's most progressive labour laws. In 2016, it famously introduced a widespread experiment to shorten the working day from eight to six hours, in order to increase productivity and workplace satisfaction, and allow people to spend more time with their families.

If that weren't enough, though, in Swedish offices there is an important tradition of taking a break to have a cup of something strong and a slice of something nice. When you want a break from your work and get up to make a cup of tea or coffee and help yourself to some cake, just let people know that you're going for your *fika*. That's a coffee and cake break in the office.

FREDAGSMYS [noun] /FRE-dags-muuss/

Friday nights in the UK are one of the most important in the week. From 4 p.m. onwards people start piling out of offices with their ties loosened and top buttons undone and falling into the nearest pub. They will stand around awkwardly for hours inhaling beers with their colleagues from mid afternoon until around midnight, when they'll finally be kicked out and sent home to collapse and wake up the next morning, probably still in their work clothes, having not made it off the couch.

In Sweden, as in other parts of Europe, weekends are a slightly different affair. In Sweden you leave your office at an extremely civilised time and go home, relax, maybe assemble some furniture and prepare some food and drinks for the evening. Then, your friends will come round, you'll dim the lights slightly and put on a nice mood music playlist from Sweden's other great gift to the world, Spotify. You'll sit and discuss the meaning of life in an informal and comfortable setting over a glass of wine and some nice food, before retiring to a beautifully minimalist sofa where you'll continue your discussion. This tradition of gathering informally at someone's house on a Friday evening to have some food and drink is called *Fredagsmys*.

KLÄMDAG [noun] /KLEM-dag/

Unlike in the UK, but like in the rest of Europe, Swedish national holidays are held on the actual day that the holiday takes place, not on the nearest Monday. This means you can't always make a long weekend of it, and sometimes you'll be left with the awkward position of working Monday to Wednesday, having Thursday off and then having to go back into the office on Friday before going home again for the actual weekend.

Spanish has the word *puente*, which is when you take the Friday off too and have a weekend so long that it's longer than the actual week. In Sweden, however, that Friday is still a working day that annoyingly sits in the middle of all the fun. It is called *klämdag*.

BJÖRNTJÄNST [noun]   /BYERNT-yenst/

It's useful in life to always assume that people generally mean well. When someone offers to help you carry your new vase from your electric car into your flat-pack energy-efficient suburban home, it's a sign of their kindness and goodwill. You should say thank you, because they're doing you a huge favour. If, however, while carrying that brand new vase they trip over something and the vase goes flying and smashes, you might not always feel like thanking them.

It's the thought that counts, though. These things happen. Sometimes you try to help someone, but in doing so just end up making things a million times worse. The Swedish language has a word to describe this phenomenon. When you try to do someone a favour that ends up having unexpected negative consequences, in Swedish you'd call that a *björntjänst*. Literally, this means a 'bear favour'.

PÅ BIT [phrase]   /PAW bit/

If you're the sort of person who likes putting a little bit of sugar in your coffee but never too much, what on Earth do you do when you're presented with a bowl full of sugar cubes? How will you break them down into something more palatable? Will you try to karate chop it down the middle with a spoon? Or will you ask the waiter to bring you a sharp knife?

In Sweden, you could instead try something called *på bit*. Rather than dissolving the sugar cube directly into your coffee, just hold it between your teeth and let the coffee wash through every time you have a sip. There's a chance you might totally rot your teeth out, though, so caution is to be advised with this one.

PÅ TÅR [phrase] / paw TAWR/

Coffee, like most things in Sweden, is not cheap, but is made up for by the fact that you can get free refills in almost all places (as long as you're ordering the filter coffee, that is). You can happily spend a large part of the day in any café getting refills and endless amounts of ice-cold water, without any fear of anyone trying to move you on or asking you to order more things. That satisfyingly free second refill of coffee is called a *på tår*.

OLLNING / SNIGLING [noun]   /OLL-ning/ / /SNIG-ling/

In a similar vein to the Dutch *swaffelen*, the Swedish word *ollning* is when men mark their territory by rubbing their genitalia against an object. Yet in the interests of gender equality, in Swedish there is a word for women who want to do the same thing: *snigling*.

OKYNNESÄTA [verb]   /OH-kuun-ne-sehh-ta/

There are three distinct stages to each trip to IKEA. The first place you should visit is the restaurant; there you can fill yourself up with delicious Swedish meatballs with mashed potato, gravy and lingonberry jam. This will give you the energy and strength you will need to spend the next few hours going through the showroom and warehouse losing those stubby little pencils and trying in vain to find precisely the right set of bookshelves that you were sure you wrote the correct number down for.

The next stage is the slightly painful process of lugging everything to the till and unceremoniously handing over the greater part of your paycheck.

The final stage, just before you start to pack everything into your car and begin the treacherous journey home without being able to see through the back window, is to run to the snack section just by the exit. There you can stuff yourself some more with ice cream and hot dogs with mustard and fried onions, even though you're still quite full from the meatballs.

That final stage is the joy of eating in Sweden. In Swedish, when you keep eating even though you're full and just because you can, that is called *okynnesäta*.

GRÅTRUNKA [verb]   /GRAWT-roon-kah/

Sometimes life can be pretty overwhelming and emotional. You're happy, but you're sad. You're excited, but you're scared. You're bored, but you're engaged. You're asleep, but you're awake. You're masturbating, but you're crying.

If you've ever experienced the last of these and wondered whether there was a word for it, you're in luck. In Swedish that is called *gråtrunka*.

SAMBO [noun]   /SAM-boh/

Sweden is one of the few countries in Europe where the majority of children are born out of wedlock. People in Sweden have a relaxed attitude to such things and as a result families in Sweden take many different forms, one of which is the traditional 'married with 2.4 kids' model that we might think of.

Sweden also has the highest number of people who live together with their long-term partners, but without being married. In Swedish there's a special word for this: *sambo*.

ZLATANERA [verb] /ZLUT-unn-eh-rah/

Sweden is a multicultural country, with almost a quarter of its population having been born overseas. Sweden has been welcoming people from other parts of Europe, such as Greece, Turkey and Italy, for about fifty years. Then, with the Yugoslav wars in the 1990s, Sweden took in a large number of refugees from Bosnia, Serbia and Croatia too. Most recently, many refugees fled war-torn Syria and the Middle East to start a new life in Europe. Alongside Germany, Sweden was their most favoured destination, meaning Syrians are now the largest immigrant group in Sweden today.

Nowadays, many of Sweden's immigrants and their descendants have been successfully integrated into the fabric of Swedish society. One of the most famous examples is Sweden's star football player, Zlatan Ibrahimović; his family came to Sweden from the Balkans, and he quickly rose to become one of the greatest football players in the world. The Swedes love him so much, they even created a whole verb based on his name: *zlatanera*. This means to dominate something, to clear something with force, just like how Zlatan shoots a goal.

TJEYLYSSNA [verb] /TYAY-luss-nah/

When you have a new song that you like, all you want to do is listen to it again and again and again on loop. You'll listen to it in the car, on the bus, before you go to sleep, while you're in the shower, while you're cooking, while you're on your *fika* and everywhere else too. For days, weeks and months, that song becomes the soundtrack to your life and fills every second of every minute of your waking life.

In Swedish when you keep listening to a song over and over again, there's a special word for it. In Swedish it's called *tjeylyssna*, which literally means 'girl listening'.

///

MYSA [verb]   /MUU-sah/

Scandinavia is famous the world over for its fantastic feel for interior design. It doesn't matter what kind of building, or where you are, when you step into a Scandinavian environment you just relax and feel at home. The Danes gave the word *hygge*, which means that fuzzy feeling you get when you feel at peace in a warm place, but the concept is similar across Scandinavia, even if it has different names in different countries.

Sweden is so far north that it has incredibly long days in the summer, where the sun barely even sets over the horizon at night, and long, arduously dark days in the winter, where you might go for weeks without even really seeing the sun. In that time of year, when the thought of being outside is so ghastly, it's absolutely essential that you have a place inside where you can feel happy, cosy and warm.

Anywhere you get that fuzzy feeling that makes you want to take your shoes off, find some nice slippers and curl up by the fire with a good book is where you'll need this next Swedish word. *Mysa* is a Swedish verb that means 'to be cosy, comfortable, warm and at peace'.

Polish

After English, the language that you're most likely to hear spoken on the streets of England is Polish. More than half a million people in the UK speak Polish as a first language, according to the 2011 census, and since Britain started welcoming Polish citizens coming to work and settle on its shores in 2004, Polish has had a visible impact on the landscape of cities, towns and villages across the country.

In just over a decade, a bond has grown between Poland and the UK which makes the two countries inseparable. Millions of young Polish people have spent their formative years in the UK working, studying and learning English, travelling freely between the two and spreading the cultures of both on either side. Nowadays, seeing cars with Polish number plates on the streets of Britain is as common as seeing cars in Poland with the steering wheel on the right-hand side. A whole generation of children has grown up bilingually, speaking English at nursery and at school and going home to speak Polish with their parents. And as much as we might think that life in the UK has been impacted by this, it pales in comparison to the difference this link has made to Poland, as people return from the UK with savings, language skills, new perspectives and fresh ideas.

The speed and extent to which this has happened has taken many by surprise, including those in government at the time, who famously estimated that only a fraction of those who arrived after 2004 would come. In recent years, Polish residents of the UK have come under a lot of undue pressure and scrutiny from people using them as a scapegoat to push a political agenda. Despite its size, sadly the Polish community remains one of the most widely misunderstood in the country. Yet hearing Polish and seeing *Polski Sklep* shops on the high street has become part of the fabric of British life, and no matter what happens that is unlikely to change any time soon.

Poland is an enormous country in Eastern Europe, whose history has largely been shaped by the fact that it is sandwiched between two even bigger countries – Germany to the west and Russia to the east. For hundreds of years Poland was subjected to occupation by other powers, leading to divisions and the Polish language being suppressed. Yet despite this Polish flourished, nowadays boasting an impressively large literary canon and around 55 million native speakers. It is a Western Slavic language, closely related to Czech and Slovak and, in a sign of the country's deeply Catholic roots, it uses the Latin alphabet.

For English speakers, trying to read Polish signs is one of the most baffling things you can do. Polish is characterised by having great long words filled with letters that are pronounced in a totally different way in English, often adorned with unfamiliar accents and symbols to represent sounds that English simply doesn't have. When Polish adopted Latin around the twelfth century Polish people quickly found that the alphabet was ill-equipped to deal with the variety of different sounds in Polish that did not exist in other languages. As a result, Polish started using combinations of letters to represent them, such as 'rz', which is like the 'zh' sound in 'leisure', or 'szcz' which is like the middle four letters of the phrase 'cash cheque'. More confusingly, Polish 'w' is pronounced like English 'v', and Polish 'ł' is like an English 'w', which creates amusing scenes as English people try to pronounce place names like *Łodż* ('wudge') or phrases like *wszystko w porządku* ('fshistko fpozhontku'), which means 'everything's OK'.

The Polish language has a unique story to tell, which reflects Poland's unique history. Perhaps what makes it most interesting is that nowadays, across Europe and the world in general, it's a language that you might find yourself needing more and more of!

POGODNIE [noun]   /poh-GOH-dnyeh/

Despite the fact that we in the UK have a reputation in other parts of the world for being slightly obsessed with the weather, our vocabulary can at times feel slightly sparse in comparison with the word choices available in other languages. We have sunny days, grey days, beautiful days, rainy days, but nothing really in between. What if the weather is not particularly wonderful, but at the same time it's not the most miserable day you've ever seen in your life either? What if the weather's just fine, pleasant and fairly unremarkable?

Fortunately, Polish has this one covered. For those days when the weather is perfectly nice but nothing extraordinary, you can say *pogodnie*.

KILKANAŚCIE [noun]   /kil-kah-NASH-tsyeh/

When talking about numbers in English, our hands are tied. We are either forced to be extremely precise and name the exact number that something is, perhaps defending ourselves slightly by adding on the phrase 'more or less', or we can use a completely indeterminable number like 'umpteen', which no one really understands, but everyone knows that it means quite a lot. But what if the number that you've got in your head is not quite as vague as 'umpteen', but not a precise figure either? What if it sits somewhere within a range of numbers, say, from twelve to nineteen?

If you're ever faced with this dilemma, once again Polish will help you out. The word *kilkanaście* means an undefined number that is greater than twelve, but less than nineteen. Never again will you be at a loss when trying to overcome the problem of vague numeracy.

JAWA [noun]   /YAH-vah/

States of consciousness and sleep are an unforgivingly binary affair in English. We can be awake, or we can be asleep. We can be conscious, or we can be unconscious. There's no in-between and there is certainly no grey area. However, as anyone who has ever slept before will recognise, there are of course other states too, when you're not quite one and not quite the other either. When you lie in bed awake with your eyes shut and, although you're not quite fully awake, you're conscious of things going on around you. You hear sounds, your senses kick back into gear and maybe you're still drifting off every now and then, but neither asleep nor awake quite cuts it. What on Earth would you call that in English?

Polish solves this problem by having a word to describe precisely that in-between state of not quite being asleep but being conscious. In Polish, that grey area between the two is called *jawa*.

PRZYMYKAĆ [verb]   /pshi-MIK-ach/

Our next Polish word once again identifies one of those grey areas of life that English has seemed to have missed out slightly. Apart from 'closing' a door and 'opening' it, what verb would you use for when you want to close the door, but also leave it slightly open? What if you want there to be a little gap, which is the universal office sign for 'I'm busy, but I'm in my office and if you want to come in and have a chat, feel free to give me a knock'? We have ways of describing around this word in English, like 'leave the door ajar' or 'put the door to', but none of them even remotely compare to Polish's impressively efficient word which means precisely all of those things, but entirely on its own.

That word is *przymykać*. To close something but also leave a tiny gap to show that it's still open.

///

POPRAWINY [noun]   /poh-prah-VI-ni/

In Poland, weddings are large affairs. People tend not to just turn up slightly shyly at their local registry office with a handful of friends and then head down to the local curry house to celebrate the start of their lives together. People throw huge parties, inviting an enormous number of guests, ranging from family and friends to colleagues, distant acquaintances and as many different people as they can manage. People put on huge spreads of wonderful Polish food and vodka and make sure that it really is an occasion to remember.

Sometimes, people put together so much food and so much vodka that even by inviting all the guests in the world, they still can't get through it all. And as throwing away food and drink is very much a cultural taboo, as it is across Central and Eastern Europe, in Poland people might come back the next day and throw a whole new party to make sure everything gets finished off. This wonderful tradition, which means that the party never really has to end, has got its own name: *poprawiny*, which you might loosely translate as an 'after party', but definitely refers to finishing everything off again the next day.

CZYTADŁO [noun]   /chi-TAD-woh/

Everyone should be able to admit to having read a *czytadło* at least once in their lives. They're the kind of thing you might pick up at the airport before an interminably long flight. You might find them lying around in a guesthouse somewhere, left by a well-meaning guest in case anyone else wants to have a read. They will come in big, bright and bold covers where the author's name stands out like the Hollywood sign, so while you're reading through it everyone around you can see exactly what you're reading and knows what to get next time they pass by a bookshop. But who cares? Reading doesn't always have to be a brain-squeezingly intellectual activity. Reading should be about pleasure too, so go find yourself a *czytadło* and enjoy yourself.

The Polish word *czytadło*, of course, means an airport thriller, a page turner, a gossip magazine, anything that gives you an enormous amount of guilty pleasure about reading, but that has next to no intellectual value whatsoever.

KOPANINA [noun]   /koh-pah-NEE-nah/

Lovers of football will be extremely grateful for this word. Those who don't like football may be nonplussed, as for them every football match is a *kopanina*. But for those who do spend their evenings flicking through all of their cable sports channels to try to find a football match, *any* football match between *any* teams at all, just to be able to watch some football, every now and then they'll find themselves having to settle for a *kopanina*.

That's the kind of match where the result is published nowhere, makes no ripples and, apart from a handful of people in two respective tiny towns somewhere in the middle of nowhere, you can be almost certain that nobody else is watching it either.

A *kopanina* is a football match of absolutely no interest, between two low-grade teams, that really is not that much fun to watch at all. In fact, it's positively boring watching two terrible teams try to kick a ball around the pitch but failing to get a goal. A *kopanina* will probably end 0–0, or if you're lucky 1–1. Just hope it doesn't go to penalties …

SIADŁO [noun]   /SYAD-woh/

Sometimes these sorts of things are hard to predict. You might flick through the channels and think you've stumbled across the *kopanina* to end all *kopanina*s, but then at the last minute things might start getting interesting. A couple of goals might come out of nowhere, the crowd will get excited and all of a sudden, you're watching the greatest football match of the century. That would be a *siadło*.

Equally, you might sit an exam that you've been dreading for months. You've been revising endlessly, but for some reason the information just doesn't seem to stick. You can't make your brain remember it, let alone understand it. But then when you get into the exam room and open the paper, you realise that actually it's fairly straightforward. You get to make all of the points you wanted to, and when you get the results you've aced it! That's also a *siadło*.

A *siadło* is an endlessly useful Polish word which means when you expect something to go very badly, but in fact it goes extremely well.

PRZYDUPAS [noun]   /pshi-du-PASS/

Our next Polish word refers to a very specific type of person. This kind of person likes to hang about, twiddling their thumbs, at the end of the working day because they know that there's a plan to go for an after-work pint and someone's bringing a company card. They're the kind of people who you invite round for a cup of coffee in the afternoon, but at 7 p.m. they're still there, smiling sweetly and safely in the knowledge that the moment you put food on the table for your family, you're going to invite them to pull up a chair and join you rather than chase them away. They're the kind of people who see an invite to a wedding as an opportunity for a free meal and will hang around forming dubiously profound friendships in order to try to squeeze those invitations out of you. And they're most certainly the kind of people that at all costs you should try to avoid.

The *przydupas* is a wonderful Polish word for someone who lingers slightly longer than perhaps they should, precisely because they know they're going to get something out of it.

KOMBINOWAĆ [verb]   /kom-BEE-no-vach/

After the Second World War, Poland found itself in the heart of the communist Eastern bloc of countries under Soviet influence. That meant that, unavoidably, it also was burdened with an incredibly complex system of bureaucracy, the legacy of which is still visible in some aspects of life there today. Sometimes, the reality of living with this kind of bureaucracy can really get you down. Why can't you just be allowed to do the things that you want to do and get the documents you need to get without all sorts of stamps, fees, queues, appointments and all sorts of other horrendous nightmares that seem largely to have passed us in the UK by?

Every now and then you might get a breakthrough. You might manage to get something done, but the hard truth is that much of your life will be spent dreaming of those moments. You'll visualise the light at the end of the bureaucratic tunnel when you're finally allowed to do exactly what you wanted, in the way you wanted. In the meantime, though, you'll just have to keep planning and keep plotting. That's where you might need the Polish word *kombinować*, which means to spend time trying to defeat the system.

ZALATWIĆ [verb]   /zah-LAT-vich/

One of the keys to breaking the endless cycle of *kombinować* is sometimes to think a little bit outside the box. There's a system, it's impregnable, it's unnecessarily complex and silly, but people live with this all over the world and they get by. The trick is simply to know how it is that you live with it and what you need to do. That's precisely where our next word comes in handy.

In the old days it was commonly known that the key to getting across some borders and into some countries was just to slip a little banknote into the inside cover of your passport. Many problems could be overcome that way, and it turns out money is a great way to make people look the other way. There are places where if you get caught speeding, you have a small wad of banknotes in your glove compartment to help solve whatever problem a traffic cop might cause for you. And, of course, if you don't have any money to hand, a simple phone call to someone in the right place might be all it takes to get you out of a sticky situation. This whole concept is captured by our next Polish word: *zalatwić*, which means to get something done through bribery or connections.

FUSZKA [noun] /FOOSH-kah/

When you have to live with an overbearingly complex and unpredictable bureaucratic system, you have to get good at learning to work with it. That means that sometimes you get pushed into certain grey areas of the law and you have to become comfortable with doing so. While in the West this idea may seem even unthinkable, in other parts of the world people take a much more realistic view of these sorts of issues and feel much more comfortable in the grey areas of the law.

One of these things is when you do a job that is not strictly legal – let's say, it's slightly under the table in terms of how you get paid, and perhaps you've not been fully registered with the relevant authorities so they're not really aware of your employment. In Polish, that kind of illegal work is called a *fuszka*.

SINY [adjective]   /SEE-nih/

There are some places in the world where people can hardly wait to grow old. The thought of being able to spend your days going down to pick up the newspaper from the shop, with people politely holding doors open for you and calling you 'sir' and treating you with respect, is of great appeal. You can see all your friends down in the local café and gossip about neighbours, football, politics or anything that tickles your fancy.

However, there is of course a much less glamorous side to ageing. You start to slow down, you find it harder to do things that you were always able to do before and, well, you age. One of the side effects of that can be a light blue, greenish, greyish shade that can start appearing on your skin to really give you that aged look. Now what on Earth would we call that colour? Fortunately, the Polish language has worked this one out and has got a word for it: *siny*.

FORMACJA [noun]   /for-MAH-tsyah/

Why do generations seem to go through certain trends? Why did people use to walk around town with their jeans around their knees? Why, lately, is everyone so obsessed with vintage to the point of actually trying to redecorate their houses to look like something only their granny and grandpa would want to live in?

Generations don't just go through fads, though. They have entire worldviews that are born and die with them, and that really become a way to tell people from two different eras apart. There's the generation of the stiff upper lip that lived through the war and for whom nothing could ever really shake them any more. There are the baby boomers with their lust for property ownership and, more recently, technology and social media. There are the millennials who believe in environmental sustainability, open-mindedness and liberalism. Where do these ideas come from and why do certain generations cling on to them, when others reject them?

Polish sees this quite simply as a single word. An idea, a belief and a worldview that persists particularly among people from a certain generation is called a *formacja*.

ŻAL [noun]   /zhal/

What do we say when we're unhappy? In English, we can say we're unhappy or we can say that we're sad. But those two words are a wonderful way to do what we do so well, which is deflect the attention of whoever we're talking to most definitely away from what the real issue is. Why are you unhappy? What has made you unhappy? And what can someone do to console you and set you back on the right track towards feeling happy again?

When Polish speakers are unhappy, they have the option of providing slightly more background information which can help others to in turn help you. They can do this with a single word, which tells someone not just that you're sad, but that you're sad because you feel that someone has let you down, disappointed or betrayed you. That word is *żal*.

NAPOIĆ [verb]   /nah-POH-eech/

In English we have a lot of words that refer to consumption of food or drink. We can 'drink', we can 'sip', we can 'slurp', we can 'guzzle', we can 'down' something, we can 'wolf something down' … there are all sorts of wonderful images that really convey just how much or how little we're enjoying whatever it is we have in front of us. We also have the word 'feed', which indicates not that we're eating, but that we're giving food to someone else to eat, which they're then enjoying.

But what on Earth do you say if you're not giving someone food, you're giving them something to drink? The phrase 'we've been fed and watered' sounds almost so ridiculous that it can only ever be used euphemistically, or in jest. One serious gap in the English language seems to be that we really do have no equivalent of 'to feed' but for drinks.

That's not a problem in Polish though: *napoić* means 'to give someone something to drink'.

Russian

Russia is a land that is shrouded in mystery. It is split between Europe and Asia, yet the vast majority of its population lives in the European side, no further from the UK than Greece, Cyprus or the Canary Islands. Most of what people know about Russia comes from its depiction in spy films, featuring villains with accents as thick as their eyebrows and hearts as cold as the icy snow outside.

But life in Russia is a great deal more complex than just what might meet the eye. Beyond the stereotypes, Russia is a unique country where everything is in a constant state of transition. The weather is forever oscillating between the freezing cold winter and the roasting hot summer. Society is coming to terms with how to match its largely conservative traditions to its modern reality, with divided opinions and mixed feelings about its memories of nearly a century of communism in the meantime. And everything that takes place in Russia does so against the backdrop of deep-rooted and ancient superstitions.

When visiting Russia, you will notice a series of unwritten but closely adhered-to rules. Nobody whistles inside. Before a long journey, everyone will take a moment to sit down together in silence before setting off. Nobody cuts their fingernails on the day of their exams. And if, heaven forbid, you have to return home because you've forgotten something, you must look in the mirror before setting off again to make sure you've successfully warded off any bad omens.

Much tension in Russian society has been caused by these deep-seated beliefs colliding with the practical aspects of modern life. Russia boasts one of the greatest literary canons of any language in the world, and the conflict between Russia's Eastern heart and Western mind forms one of its central themes. The Russian language, therefore, has been shaped by this issue and has had to adapt to become the vehicle for communicating Russia's unique circumstances and way of life. Unfortunately, many of the more stylised translations of Dostoevsky, Tolstoy, Gogol, Pushkin and Turgenev are forced to sacrifice the nuances of the Russian original, which only Russian speakers will truly be able to appreciate.

Several grammatical features make Russian quite special from a linguistic point of view and lead people to make mistakes when speaking English that have become trademark ways in which to spot a Russian speaker. Notably, there is no word for 'the' or 'a' in Russian, so Russian speakers commonly miss it out in English. There is also no form of the verb 'to be' in the present tense in Russian. As a result, instead of saying 'The tea is very hot', a Russian might say 'Tea very hot!'

Russian is also a language that is very keen on details. It is one of the few languages where you can buy a whole textbook, of substantial length, solely on the topic of how to say the verb 'to go'. Depending on whether you are going by foot or by vehicle, out of habit or by chance, and whether you intend to stay there or come back, or make the journey several times, you would in each case have to use an entirely different Russian word.

Precision is perhaps the word that most strongly comes to mind when thinking of how to describe the Russian language. Yet, as a result of that, Russian is bursting with words that perceptively capture so much of the nuance of life that simply passes other languages by.

ОДНОЛЮБ / ADNALYÚB [noun]   /ad-nah-LYUB/

Our first Russian word is about love. Russians are very in touch with their emotional sides, with a deep-seated belief in the power of the soul, of fate and of intangible forces that only show themselves through unshakeable superstitions. Love, of course, is very much a part of that, hence the word однолюб (*adnalyúb*).

If someone is an однолюб, then they're not going to be looking around at other people on the trolleybus or going behind your back to have affairs on those long, cold winter nights. If you've found yourself an однолюб, then you have hit the jackpot. No matter what happens, your однолюб will stay and be there for you entirely unconditionally. Because someone who is an однолюб will only ever love once in their life, which is what the word literally means: 'one-love'.

ПЕРЕПОДВЫПОДВЕРТ / PEREPODVYPODVYÉRT [noun]
/pyeh-ryeh-pad-VUY-pad-vyert/

Political relations between Russia and the West have been rocky in recent years. Despite much hope that they would grow closer after the end of communism and the Cold War, sadly the two worlds seem to be drifting further apart. As the West becomes more secular, Russia becomes more religious. The West strongly criticises Russia for its record on press freedom, while Russia accuses the West of hypocrisy and complex geopolitical self-interest. As politicians seem determined to drive a wedge between the two, perhaps Western leaders would benefit from adopting a certain Russian word, in order to help better understand their rationale.

Russians love to be enigmatic, and no word better summarises this than the word переподвыподверт (*perepodvypodvyért*). You could say that you do something с переподвыподвертом (*s perepodvypodvyértom*), or 'with' this word, which essentially means that you do something in an unbelievably complex and entirely incomprehensible way. You may get it done and get great results, but the point is that to any onlookers, how you got there is a total mystery.

But as they say in Russian, 'на вкус и цвет товарищов нет' ('*na fkooss ee tsvyet tavárishchov nyet*') – 'in taste and colour there are no comrades'. Or as Russians would wryly translate it: 'tastes differ'.

БЕСПРЕДЕЛ / BYESPREDYÉL [noun]   /byes-pryeh-DYEL/

There are two types of people in life. There are those who keep their heads down and get on with life, being courteous and polite to their fellow citizens and never really causing any problems for anyone. And then there are those who are totally off the wall. They do crazy things, like putting brightly coloured socks on their faces and singing punk songs in cathedrals in central Moscow (yes Pussy Riot – we're looking at you). They nail sensitive parts of their anatomy to the freezing cold cobblestones of Red Square. They run through exclusive shopping centres as naked as the day they were born, calling for gender equality. What on Earth is it that makes these people tick?

Well, the Russian language has a very special word reserved for this kind of behaviour. People who act like this, against the norms and rules of society, are doing so because they are simply without any pre-set limits, without any boundaries or laws. In other words, they are беспредел (*byespredyél*), or 'without limits', and are happiest when wreaking havoc in the name of a cause on an otherwise unremarkably sleepy snowy day in the Russian capital.

ПОЧЕМУЧКА / PACHEMÚCHKA [noun]   /pah-cheh-MOOCH-kah/

Why is the sky blue? Why does the week only have seven days in it? Why do cows go 'moo'? Why do some people insist on asking so many questions and never seem satisfied with the answer 'because'? We all know that 2- and 3-year-olds are famous questioners, as they set out in the world and start really exploring it for the first time, it's natural for them to want a lot of answers. It's just that some people become adults and still don't seem to really grasp that there aren't always answers to everything and that in fact the world is a confusing, complex and inexplicable sort of place that you just have to make do with.

Fortunately, Russian has a word for those sorts of people. If someone asks you a lot of questions and never really seems satisfied with the answer, then they are a почемучка (*pachemúchka*), which comes from the word почему (*pachemú*) meaning 'why'.

Be wary of being a почемучка, though. What's that English expression about curiosity and the cat?

БЕЛОРУЧКА / BYELARÚCHKA [noun]   /byel-ah-ROOCH-kah/

All of us know someone who's reluctant to help out with certain jobs. Ask them to take the rubbish out and they'll freeze. Ask them to clean the shower head and they'll go very pale. Don't even think of asking them to clean the toilet, as you can guess what the answer will be.

Some people simply think they're too good for those kinds of chores. For some reason they just don't believe that they have it in them to pull on a pair of brightly coloured rubber gloves and get elbow deep in some horrible grimy muck and get rid of it all. They'll tell you that it's not their strength, that they're really much more of a mind-over-matter kind of person. They'll tell you anything to get out of what you're asking them to do, but the real reason is that they think they're too good for dirty work and won't pull their weight.

If you're one of those people though, there's bad news. The Russian language is on to you and has come up with a whole word just for you: белоручка (*byelarúchka*), which means a 'white-handed-person'.

НАДРЫВ / NADRÝV [noun]   /nad-RUYV/

We in the UK are infamous for holding our tongues. We freely advertise to the world that we have long succeeded in transforming our upper lips into impenetrable stiff steel doors that keep all of our emotions locked up and safely far away from anyone else. That's why we just keep calm and carry on, because what else would you want to do? Don't even think about making a scene – that's the only thing that could make things worse!

However, no matter how high, how strong, or how high-tech, no fortifications are ever strong enough to keep things in (or out) all the time. Every now and then, you might have a little moment and suddenly, entirely unwittingly, blurt out what you really think and then spend a panicked few minutes trying desperately to work out how to put it all back in your mouth, before realising with horror that you can't. Don't worry though, Russian has got your back for these moments. The writer Dostoevsky actually coined this one: надрыв (*nadrýv*). This is an uncontrollable emotional outburst in which your true feelings are actually revealed.

САМОРОДОК / SAMARÓDOK [noun]   /sah-mah-ROH-dak/

Some people do a great job of seeming smart. They can talk the talk, they can walk the walk, and they probably learned to do all of those things in a very prestigious institution where they received an outstanding education that will serve them for the rest of their lives. But that doesn't necessarily mean that they actually are all that smart. In fact, quite the opposite could be the case, and if it hadn't been for their education things might have turned out very differently.

But then you get the opposite. You get the people who didn't get a good education, who didn't have the means to go to university and might not even have finished school. Yet when you speak to those people, you quickly realise they're as sharp and as quick as anything. They read books, they self-educate and they can hold a conversation on anything as well as any university graduate.

Those are the people who brought themselves up. Russian calls them самородок (*samaródok*), which literally means 'self-grower'.

АВОСЬКА / AVÓSSKA [noun]   /ah-VOSS-kah/

Because of Russians' deep-rooted cultural belief in fate, they believe anything could happen at any time. Things can happen that are totally out of the ordinary and there's not much you can do about them, except be prepared at all times for all eventualities. They call this constant unpredictable nature of life авось (*avóss*).

In the Soviet Union, it was very common for there to be food shortages in shops. You would go to buy things but never really be sure what was on the shelves. Most of the time, there wasn't much. You couldn't rely on there being fish, or meat, or anything really. You just had to make do with what you could find.

But every now and then, thanks to авось, there would be a miracle and word would spread round town that a certain shop had some fish. Quickly the queues would form around the block, as everyone knew that supply was limited and could run out at any time.

As people stood in these queues, they would reach into their bags and pull out an авоська (*avósska*). This was a spare string bag that could fold up so small that you could carry it around everywhere with you, just in case you happened upon a shop that had something you wanted.

Nowadays in the West when we have to remember to take a bag with us to the supermarket and pay extra for any plastic bags we use, perhaps the word авоська is just about ready to make a comeback.

ГОЛОЛЕДНИЦА / GALALYÉDNITSA [noun]   /gah-lah-LYED-nee-tsah/

During the Russian winter it's more than normal for temperatures to fall well below freezing, with several metres of snowfall covering railway lines, runways, pavements, roads and balconies. All of these are rather nonchalantly cleaned up at breathtaking speed and the country carries on entirely unfazed. Meanwhile, in the UK even just a faint rumour of snow can cause motorways to be shut, flights to be stranded and a nation of delighted children to wake up to the news that for some reason the schools are shut.

As a result, Russia has developed a very complex and detailed understanding of snow, of ice and of the climate it has. That gives rise to words like гололедница (*galalyédnitsa*), which literally means a 'naked sheet of ice'. This is a layer of ice which settles, then as temperatures rise will melt again, and then as temperatures drop again will refreeze, creating treacherous conditions on the road.

НЕНАГЛЯДНЫЙ / NYENAGLYÁDNIY [adjective] /nye-nah-GLYAD-nuy/

One of Russia's most intriguing cultural exports is the world-famous Fabergé egg. These impressively glamourous decorated eggs were created by House of Fabergé in St Petersburg in the mid-nineteenth century for the tsars, who with their residences in places like the Winter Palace and other obscenely large and beautiful palaces had a taste for the decadent. They are generally made from gold, decorated with all sorts of precious stones and jewels, and exquisitely painted so that they can be put on display for any guests that come to pay a visit. The practice borrows from the Orthodox tradition of painting eggs at Easter.

It's said that these Fabergé eggs are so precious and so exquisite that often they cannot even be looked at directly. They create in the beholder such a sense of inadequateness and imperfection in the shadow of their beauty, that beholders cannot even bring it upon themselves to cast their eyes upon them. This gives us the Russian word ненаглядный (*nyenaglyádniy*), which literally means something that is so precious that it 'cannot be looked at'.

ЗАПОЙ / ZAPÓY [noun]   /zah-POY/

Alcohol consumption in Europe is among the highest in the world, with Russia near the top. This might not be surprising given that Russia only classified beer as alcoholic in 2011 (previously, anything under 10 per cent alcohol content was considered a foodstuff).

In recent years huge efforts have been made in Russia to reverse the trend of alcoholism, with initiatives around raising taxes and banning the sale of alcohol at night proving reasonably successful. Nevertheless, Russian still contains a considerable number of words that are just about drinking. Here's the first of these in this chapter: запой (*zapóy*), which is when you embark not just on a heavy night or a bit of a bender, but several consecutive days of heavy drinking.

ПРОПИТЬ / PRAPIT [verb]   /prah-PEET/

Sometimes you have moments when you just question everything and decide to make drastic and spontaneous decisions, like selling your TV, your car or your house. We all need a fresh start sometimes, so why not get rid of the things that are weighing us down the most?

That's fine and, of course, fairly normal. What you do next, though, is where this word might come in handy. If you have someone round to inspect your TV, help them down the stairs with it and put it in the back of their car, count the cash they hand over to you from it and then find yourself immediately heading straight off to the nearest open drinking establishment and then spending all of that cash on drinking, then in Russian you'd use the special word пропить (*prapít*). This literally means to 'drink through' something and is certainly not the most sensible way to spend money.

НЕДОПЕРЕПИЛ / NYEDAPEREPÍL [verb]   /nye-dah-pyeh-ryeh-PEEL/

We've all been there. We've all had nights where we've drunk slightly too much, or perhaps a bit more than slightly too much, and suddenly the evening's over. Your responsible friends will bundle you into the back of a taxi and send you home, where you can suffer in private and wake up into a spinning and confusing aftermath in the morning.

But what about when you know you've drunk too much, but at the same time even then you still haven't drunk anywhere near as much as you wanted to? Your evening's been cut short by your body not being able to take it, but you had plans to drink at least three times as much as what you actually got through? That's precisely where Russian is very useful, because it has a word for exactly those awful moments: недоперепил (*nyedaperepíl*), which is when you drank too much, but still nowhere near as much as you intended to.

СУШНЯК / SOOSHNYÁK [noun]   /soosh-NYAK/

If you've had a night when you've недоперепил-ed, then in the morning there's a high chance that you're going to feel a bit worse for wear. This can be mitigated by drinking higher-quality vodka, but often we're not in a position to know whether the quality of what's on the label matches what's in the bottle. One side effect that you may also experience is that as you wake up and try to speak, you may have the sensation that the inner lining of your throat has been removed and replaced with a large container of sand that has been shipped over from the Gobi desert. Your voice is coarse, and no matter how much water you drink it just persists in being dry and hostile to any attempts you make to soothe it.

If you're in Russia, people will know what to do. You have сушняк (*sooshnyák*), which is an incredibly dry throat that follows a night of heavy drinking. Don't worry though, the Russians will have plenty of переподвыподверт home remedies at the ready to set you on the right track. Or so they say ...

ОПОХМЕЛИТЬСЯ / APAKHMYELÍTSA [verb]   /ah-pakh-myell-EET-sa/

As the old saying goes, though, 'if you can't beat them, join them'. Sometimes the only way to fight a hangover, or похмелие (*pakhmyéliye*), is just to carry on with more of the same medicine. This is commonly what foreign students on study abroad programmes in Russia are advised by their бабушка (*bábushka*), or the Russian grandma they live with, when they are suffering the next day. Get out a shot glass and fill it with some cheap, nasty white wine, then close your eyes, knock it back and think of Mother Russia. Apparently it opens the veins, or something similarly plausible.

In Russian, this is called опохмелиться (*apakhmyelítsa*) and is similar to hair of the dog but with a slight difference. It comes from the word похмелие, meaning hangover, but whenever you add the prefix 'о-' to anything in Russian, it gives it the meaning of 'to confront head on' or 'take by the horns'. So, in Russian, when you drink through a hangover you are really 'taking your hangover by the horns'.

The IPA: Learning to Read Any Language in the World

Language fans across the world were delighted when IPA started appearing in all respectable drinking establishments. Finally, they thought, the dream of having a universally readable writing system that could be applied to any language would become a reality. And who would have thought that the first frontier to be conquered would be their local pub?

However, the craze for IPA was nothing to do with linguistics, although it has become the punchline of many niche language jokes since. The IPA which we're discussing in this section of the book does not, of course, stand for 'India Pale Ale' but for 'International Phonetic Alphabet', and refers to something different to the orangey, hoppy drink you'll find all over East London. The International Phonetic Alphabet was set up in order to find a solution to a very specific problem.

One of the biggest obstacles to writing books about language like this one is to make sure that the reader knows how the words that you are including sound. Languages do not have consistent or universal writing systems, which means that letters can be pronounced totally differently and unpredictably. The letter 'r', for example, sounds in English like a toothy 'w', in French like a guttural clearance, in Spanish like a gentle drill, and in certain positions in some dialects of Portuguese even like an 'h'. Attempts have been made in this book to circumvent this problem by deploying an exaggerated anglicised transcription next to each entry, but this has clear limitations in terms of whom it would mean something to.

In the nineteenth century, the International Phonetic Association was acutely aware of this problem, and so they developed the International Phonetic Alphabet. Its aim was and is to be able to provide a transparent and universal phonetic transcription of any spoken language in the world. At first it was developed specifically within Europe for European languages, but gradually has been expanded to include as many sounds, or phonemes, as linguists have found to exist.

The English version of the IPA was completed in 1847 by Isaac Pitman and Henry Ellis, and means that we have a way of writing the English down without getting mixed up with its confusing silent consonants and irregular vowels. For example, the activity of 'reading' and the town of 'Reading' cannot be confused in IPA, for one is written 'riːdɪŋ and the other 'rɛːdɪŋ.

However, one barrier that stops people from engaging with the IPA is that some of its symbols look unfamiliar and strange. The good news is, though, that every symbol consistently represents one single sound, which means that learning to read the IPA is simply a question of memorising what each symbol means. There are also some symbols, such as the colon-like ':' which are just there to show when a sound is long, and the apostrophe ''' which denotes that the proceeding syllable is stressed.

While the IPA generally does a pretty good job, it does still have some shortcomings. One criticism is that it is inherently Eurocentric in its nature, as it was designed by European phonologists to transcribe European languages, based on existing European writing systems. This means it may not always serve African, Asian, Australian or American languages as well as it could. The other problem is that it does not conventionally convey intonation, which means that the nuance of what people are saying still can be lost.

Nonetheless, the IPA does a better job than most, and with some practice can easily be acquired so that you can understand what those little symbols mean next time you look up a word in the dictionary. As a way of getting started, here is an overview of the full range of sounds in standard British English, as represented by the IPA:

Long Vowels

i: 'ee' in 'cheese'
u: 'oo' in 'loo'
ɜ: 'er' in 'worse'
ɔ: long 'or' in 'north'
ɑ: long 'a' like in 'bath' (southern England only)

Short Vowels

ɪ   'i' in 'pick'

ʊ   'u' in 'foot'

e   'e' in 'press'

ə   'uh' in 'hungover'

æ   'a' in 'cat'

ʌ   'u' in 'hut' (south-east England mainly)

ɒ   'o' in 'porridge'

Consonants

m   'm' in 'mood'

n   'n' in 'need'

ŋ   'ng' in 'learning'

p   'p' in 'parsley'

b   'b' in 'belly'

t   't' in 'tea'

d   'd' in 'dog'

k   'k' in 'careful'

g   'g' in 'gallavant'

tʃ   'ch' in 'cherry'

dʒ   'j' in 'jelly'

f   'f' in 'favour'

v   'v' in 'Venice'

θ   'th' in 'think'

ð   'th' in 'though'

s   's' in 'sign'

z   'z' in 'zeal'

ʃ   'sh' in 'shoulder'

ʒ   'zh' in 'Asia'

h   'h' in 'healing'

l   'l' in 'like'

r   'r' in 'regret'

j   'y' in 'yes'

w   'w' in 'waste'

Diphthongs

/eɪ/   'ay' in 'day'

/aɪ/   'uy' in 'guy'

/ɔɪ/   'oy' in 'toy'

/əʊ/   'ow' in 'blow'

/aʊ/   'ou' in 'house'

/ɪə/   'eer' in 'sheer'

/eə/   'air' in 'hair'

/ʊə/   'our' in 'tour'

The above IPA is designed for transcribing Received Pronunciation (RP), which these days relatively few of us speak in the UK, unless we're related to the royal family. Therefore there are huge variations depending on different accents and dialects, which means that if you don't quite recognise one of those sounds as being one you'd make yourself, don't worry.

With the information given in the tables above, see if you can read the sentences below:

1. haʊ mʌtʃ wʊd wʊd ə ˈwʊdˌtʃʌk tʃʌk ɪf ə ˈwʊdˌtʃʌk kʊd tʃʌk wʊd?
2. ðə ˈθɜːti-θri: θiːvz θɔːt ðæt ðeɪ θrɪld ðə θrəʊn θruːˈaʊt ˈθɜːzdeɪ.
3. sɪks sliːk swɒnz swæm ˈswɪftli ˈsaʊθwədz.
4. ðə reɪn ɪn speɪn fɔːlz ˈmeɪnli ɒn ðə pleɪn.
5. ðəʊ hi: θɔːt hiːd θɔːt ɪt θruː, ðɪs ˈθʌrəli tɔːt hɪm ðæt hi: ˈhædnt.

About the Author

ALEX RAWLINGS was crowned Britain's most multilingual student in 2012 and is fluent in eleven languages. He has lived in five different countries and acts as a language ambassador, representing the UK globally and organising the annual worldwide Polyglot Conference. He has previously written *How to Speak Any Language Fluently* (Little Brown). Alex is currently Language Learner in Residence at award-winning language start-up Memrise. He lives in North London.